THE FREEDOM

SWIMMERS

Suk Hing's Story

Tony Chin

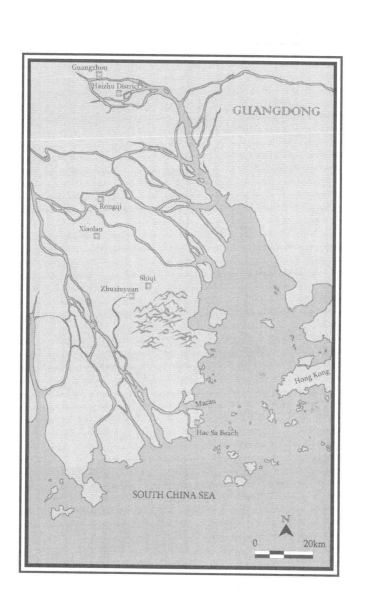

Guangzhou

Haizhu District

GUANGDONG

Rongqi

Xiaolan

Shiqi

Zhuxiuyuan

Hong Kong

Macau

Hac Sa Beach

SOUTH CHINA SEA

N

0   20km

Contents

Acknowledgements

I dedicate this book to my mother who this story is about. Without her courage, determination, and self-worth I would not be the man I am today. This book is also dedicated to my uncle and all the other dissidents that risked their lives to give themselves, their sons, daughters and generations to come a better life that they never would of had.

Also a special thank you to the lovely Sharon. Without her trusted guidance and help, this book would have never seen completion.

Prologue:

"Water can float a boat as it can capsize it"

June 6, 1966

Suk Hing felt as if the very marrow in her bones had turned to ice. At the same time, her lungs, legs, and arms were on fire. She had to take a break, to pause for a second and allow her throbbing muscles and screaming lungs to recover.

She tread water slowly, tilting her head back to inhale deep gulps of cold sea air. After catching her breath, she listened. There was nothing beyond the sea itself and the hard slap of water against her frozen body.

The sea stretched pitch black for miles in every direction. The horizon, her only guide, was itself pitching, a moving dark poised to disorient and lead her off course. A rough estimate told her that she had already been swimming for seven, maybe eight, hours.

She told herself to move, to keep pushing, that she must be almost there. There would be no one to help her now, no one to drive her on. Panic welled in her throat. She was alone. Not alone, not entirely: death was there, too. With an effort, she raised her tiny frame above the water's surface and resumed her swim. A late start meant that she was swimming against the tide. The pain in her slender limbs confirmed the extra effort needed to move her in the right direction. She thought she had been prepared, but her practice and mental resolve hadn't equipped her for the way the water constantly shifted and lapped, bobbing her about and filling her mouth with brine. She hadn't been prepared for how it would feel to lose the shoreline, how small and fragile she would become against this great force of nature, her fear of the creatures clamouring around and beneath her. She had to put those thoughts aside, and keep moving.

She lowered her head, took a deep breath, and pushed her body into the strongest front crawl she could still manage. Dawn would break soon, and she needed to be closer to her destination or everything would be lost. Lifting her head for air, she almost cried with relief. In the distance she could see city lights, burning like stars. Land wasn't far.

She swam on with renewed determination, but the lights came no closer. She dived and pushed and crawled, but the lights came no closer. If anything, they appeared more distant. The tide, she realized, was carrying her backwards. Kicking for all she was worth, she frantically tried to propel herself forward.

She broke with the dawn. Her small body could take no more. Punished and undernourished, it gave in. She had nothing left to give. She closed her eyes. It would be over soon.

She thought that she had died but the sea roar was still in her ears and the morning sun was on her skin for a moment before it was swallowed by the shadows now looming over her. The shadows made clicking noises, as though speaking in some alien, insect language. Her vision cleared and the shadows became men, young men, holding rifles.

She was back where she had started.

Chapter One

*"Wind not always favorable;
soldiers aren't always victorious"*

1947–1954

Suk Hing Lee was born in 1947, in the city of Guangzhou in Southern China. Though the end of the second World War promised stability, the country was plagued by political unrest. The decades long civil war between the Chinese Communist Party and the Kuomintang, or Nationalist, Party had come to a temporary armistice to counter the greater threat of Imperial Japan; but less than a year after the war, hostilities resumed with full force.

Even still, if Suk Hing had been old enough to take the measure of her life as it was then, she might have considered herself born lucky. Her father, Simd Sum Lee, had done very well for himself; a former high-ranking officer in the Chinese Army, Suk Hing's father had secured a lucrative post-war career as a government tax inspector. Along with her fifteen siblings and half-siblings, Suk Hing thrived under her father's affluent position. The large, grand estate in which the family lived adjoined a complex of smaller houses that accommodated not only her father's three wives and numerous offspring, but also a household staff of around twenty, from cooks to gardeners, nannies to cleaners. Both the main and surrounding houses were encircled by eight-foot high walls of ash-grey brick, partitioned by an immense wooden gate which stood at the end of a broad parkway embedded with flat slabs of orange clay. From above, the main house appeared in the shape of an 'L' whose ligature formed the left and rear walls of the property. The roof was traditional, peaked with a flat slope that curved upwards into 'flying eaves' common in the rainier south, and adorned with rounded terracotta tiles shaped like half moons. To the right of the main house lay a small grass park flecked with trees whose green, heart-shaped leaves stood in stark contrast with the pallid adobe surrounding it. The interior of this central dwelling contained a sprawling complex of dozens of rooms, into and out of which scurried Suk Hing's father's employees, dusting and polishing an assortment of ornamental decorations dating from the Ming dynasty, which the children were warned never to touch. Suk Hing's privilege and family connections afforded her a wealth of opportunities. She could have chosen whichever path in life took her fancy.

In 1949, everything changed.

On October 1st, Mao Zedong came to power, and declared the creation of the People's Republic of China. Though too young to realize it, the very things that had made Suk Hing's life comfortable, their wealth, close ties to the government, and status as feudal landlords, would make her family a prime target in the communist government's plan to radically restructure the very foundations of Chinese society.

Suk Hing's strongest memory of that time was of hearing her parents talking in hushed and urgent voices in the dead of night. Much later, she discovered that her father had been part of the first wave of officials to be ousted from their positions. He intended to build two other properties; he wanted to move his wives into separate accommodations with their respective children, so that the families would already be accommodated when, and not if, they seized the estate. She couldn't have understood then how worried her parents were about the situation, or that her father stashed money around the house in makeshift bags in order for them to continue to live, keeping the staff paid and the family fed. As far as Suk Hing knew, nothing had changed. The family still gathered together for dinner around the intricately detailed, mahogany dining table, with its marble centre and matching chairs. Their staff still scurried around taking care of the family and seeing to all its needs, and the house was still adorned with expensive ornamental decorations that she knew she must never touch or play with.

In 1952, when Suk Hing was five years old, her father disappeared. A few days later, an armed detachment of uniformed soldiers descended upon the family home, demanding to know where he had gone. Crouched in the corner, Suk Hing watched as her mother stood her ground and refused to admit any knowledge of his whereabouts.

The leader sneered. "Very well, have it your way. Men, round up these servants, they can be put to better use elsewhere. They should be working in the fields for the good of the country, not pandering to one spoiled family."

The soldiers rounded up the remaining staff and marched them from the estate, helping themselves to some of the family's more expensive household artifacts. On his way out, the leader turned once more to Suk Hing's mother. "Have no doubt, we will find him." Suk Hing knew he was referring to her father, but couldn't imagine what he might have done wrong. She knew that her father worked for the people in charge, so why were they sending these horrible men to find him?

Her mother, Nim Ping Kan, said nothing. Her features remained stoic, her body language defiant. Suk Hing ran to her as the soldiers left, seeking comfort and reassurance. She received neither. As always, her mother faced the situation with determination and practicality.

"Well, Suk Hing, it seems like we will be fending for ourselves from now on. I will have to go out to work, so you will have to take on some of the household duties now that we have no servants to handle them for us."

Suk Hing looked at her mother with wide, dark eyes. "Where's father? Will he be OK? Why do those men want him?"

"Pah, the Government!" her mother replied, with an aggressive wave of her hand. "He worked hard and well for the last one, so now he is considered a traitor to the new one, through no actions of his own. If they find him, they will arrest him."

Suk Hing didn't understand all the words, but her child's mind understood that bad men were after her father. She never saw him again.

Suk Hing's life went on, although under very different circumstances. The previously large household had shrunk to just her, her mother, and her elder brother, Kin Mou. Kin Mou was the second youngest of her full siblings, and the only other sibling still living at home. Her twenty-three-year-old brother, Li, was a fighter pilot in the army and had been gone for a long time. He would go on to fight in the Korean War, but the family never spoke of him around Suk Hing. He had left when Suk Hing was very small; she didn't really remember him. Her sixteen-year-old sister was also in the army and Suk Hing never saw her either.

Under Mao's Agrarian Reform Law of 1950, their palatial home and the property surrounding it had been confiscated. The family that did remain were restricted to but a few rooms, and the dozen or so rooms through which Suk Hing and her siblings once freely roamed were repurposed as individual apartments, filled with strangers assigned to live there by government fiat.

Suk Hing's mother had never had to work before, and now she tried to eke out a living for them by picking and selling large leaves that people used to wrap the meat and fish they purchased from the market, allowing them to carry it home. She also took in mending work, patching holes in pants and doing other sewing jobs to try to keep the family fed. When she had time, she would do beautiful embroidery work to sell. Although she'd had no formal training, Nim Ping Kan was very skilled with her hands and her work was impressive. Despite her hard work and initiative, stitching didn't bring in much in the way of money. Soon, the family found themselves short of everything from food to fuel. Now that the servants were gone, Suk Hing had to learn how to carry out household chores, and she tried to help by gathering wood for Nim Ping Kan to sell along with the leaves. The small family struggled to make ends meet and have enough food to survive. Hunger was something Suk Hing had never experienced before in her short life, but it was a feeling she soon got used to.

The highlight of the year was when Suk Hing and her mother would visit her paternal grandmother. She lived alone on a farm, her husband having died before Suk Hing was born. Unlike her mother, who refrained from terms of endearment or idle conversation, and, since the day the soldiers arrived for her father, had become even shorter tempered, Suk Hing's grandmother was a gentle, kind woman, who openly showered her granddaughter with affection.

The farm itself was a beautiful, wondrous place. It was situated on one of the intermittent plains of the Pearl River delta, whose tributaries carved the terrain like a network of veins feeding some massive, primordial hand. At high tide, the plain was flooded with two feet of delta runoff. At low tide, the receding waters would leave behind a silty, mineral-rich backwash that fed a lush grove of lychee and starfruit trees. Stocked thick with red and yellow fruit, the canopy sometimes appeared to Suk Hing like a mass of huddled umbrellas, under which she could spend entire, airy, afternoons picking and eating lychee and gazing into the flat expanse extending beyond the farm in every direction. She wished she could visit more often than once a year.

When she was seven-years-old, Suk Hing got her wish, though perhaps not in the way she had hoped. Her mother suffered a stroke. Nim Ping Kan was in the hospital for nearly three months. During her mother's illness, Suk Hing had to look after the house and her brother. At eleven-years-old, Kin Mou was the elder, but Suk Hing was the girl, and therefore expected to cook and clean for him, along with attending school and visiting her mother as often as she could. When Nim Ping Kan finally returned home, Suk Hing learned that her life was about to change dramatically again.

"Suk Hing, come sit with me, I want to speak to you."

Suk Hing eagerly went to her mother's side, glad to have her home, even if she wasn't quite well. The responsibility of running a household at her age had been a daunting task, one she hoped her mother would resume now she was home. So far, her childhood was passing by in a blur of hardship.

"You understand that I was very ill, Suk Hing?"

Suk Hing nodded solemnly. She would never forget the chill that had pierced her heart seeing her mother's face

11

twist and fall before she had collapsed. She had already lost so much; she was terrified she was going to lose her mother too. Thankfully, her mother had made a recovery of sorts, retaining most of her speech and movement, albeit weakened.

"I'm not strong enough to work much at the moment. We're going to have to live with your grandmother on the farm."

Suk Hing tried not to show her excitement, thinking that life there could only be better than the one they had now.

"Will Kin Mou come too?"

"No," her mother replied grimly. "His teacher came to visit me before I left the hospital. He has taken a liking to Kin Mou, and wanted my assurance that he would stay in school. When I told him of my plans, he became quite insistent that Kin Mou stay here in the city. He will stay in the house alone, and this teacher will keep an eye on him. Your sister has agreed to help when she can."

Suk Hing didn't dare question her mother's decision. After the stroke, Nim Ping Kan suffered frequent headaches, which had further contracted her already short temper into a fine, knife-edged point, easily agitated at even the slightest trespass. She was never much for small talk, even before the stroke; now, after all that had happened, her love for her family, though still as indestructible as diamond, came wrapped in some still harder thing whose texture made it difficult to grasp, but it was there, and Suk Hing knew it was there.

As Suk Hing contemplated the turn her life was taking, she couldn't help wonder how her brother would survive in the city on his own. However, she had no say in the decision, her mother's mind was set and Suk Hing wasn't inclined to change it. She was looking forward to the move. They were barely surviving here. She was always hungry, always tired, and things couldn't possibly be worse than they were in these few rooms haunted with memories of the family and lifestyle they had lost. Her mother wanted them to leave the next day, so Suk Hing packed up what was left of their belongings.

Chapter Two

"Vicious as a tigress can be, she never eats her own cub"

1954–1958

Suk Hing kneeled upon sea-blue pile and woven chrysanthemum and lotus frets. Her nanny, Mei, sat next to her smiling, as she took her finger and traced it along the scrolling vines set in relief on the carpet. Mei was saying something Suk Hing couldn't quite hear. Suk Hing leaned forward to catch what the voice was saying but when Mei spoke again it sounded like Nim Ping Kan's voice: "Come on, lazy bones. Time to get up."

Suk Hing groaned and rubbed her eyes. Her nanny, the carpet and flowers, evaporated into the motes of dust hovering above her bed, barely illuminated in the grey morning. She longed to lie in the comfort of her bed, absorbed in her unfiltered dreams and fall back to sleep. It took her only a moment to realize she was indeed at her grandmother's farm house and with that, all the realities of her life flitted back in. She climbed out of bed as quickly as she could, not wishing to anger her mother and start the day off badly. She needed to carry out a few household chores before she began the forty-five minute walk to school.

The walk was the downside of living in the country. In bad weather the route was treacherous, and often she would slip and fall in the deep mud, arriving at school in filthy clothes, having to endure discomfort and embarrassment until it was time to walk home. It was either that, or head to the stream, strip and wash her clothes, and put them back on soaking wet hoping she wasn't spotted. She couldn't begin to imagine what would happen if it got back to her mother that she was in her undergarments in public. Not even grandma would be able to save her from her mother's wrath then.

After the stroke, Nim Ping Kan had become not only more cross, but increasingly introspective. As young as she was, Suk Hing felt she understood the frustration that her mother was going through. She had lost her husband, her home, staff, and now the persistent headaches and physical weakness left in the stroke's aftermath had cost her the ability to work. This last privation pained Nim Ping Kan greatly; she was a proud woman with a strong work ethic and a staunch determination to survive and succeed. Suk Hing knew her mother loved her dearly and was only trying to instil the same qualities in her daughter in order for her to thrive in their new environment, so she tried to be gentle with her mother and obedient to her wishes. She often managed to make her angry though, and during these times, her mother would refuse to feed her. Confused and upset, Suk Hing would run to her grandma, who always had a kind word to soothe her and some food to give her, however little.

Food and money were still in desperate need. One of her half-sisters tried to help by sending them a small stipend each month, but it didn't go far. It had to be used to buy rice, the only staple in their restricted diet. As a farm owner, her grandmother was allowed to earn roughly 150 Yuan per year, and it wasn't enough for the family to live on. Between keeping themselves adequately fed and sending money back to the city for Kin Mou's keep and education, their meagre budget was stretched to the breaking point. The pressure it put on them was tremendous, they had little to sacrifice in the first place.

Part of Suk Hing's new routine involved a weekly four-hour excursion to the city in a stuffy, lurching shuttle bus. On Friday, she would then walk to the old house, let herself in, and begin chores in the now empty rooms that still, technically, belonged to the family. Afterwards, she would walk to the local medical clinic and make an appointment for the following week for her mother, who required frequent check-ups. In the opinion of the adults around her, the one and only thing that seemed to improve since the rise of Communism in China was the level of healthcare available. Suk Hing considered such advancements meagre when weighed against the full picture and found it difficult to be grateful. After making her mother's appointment, she would do a variety of other small errands and chores required before returning to the house and staying overnight. On Saturday, she would return home.

She never once saw her brother during these brief outings. He would be at school and wouldn't return to the house until after Suk Hing had left on Saturday. She found it strange and slightly disconcerting being all alone in the rooms allocated to them in a property that was actually theirs, unable to access places she had freely roamed such a short while ago. She never slept well on the nights she had to stay. The place seemed haunted now. Often she would wake from nightmares of leering soldiers searching the house while she cowered in the corner, not understanding. She was always so tired on Saturdays that she wished she could sleep on the journey home, but the noisy, jostling shuttle contrived to keep her awake until she would arrive home, utterly exhausted.

It was during one of these weekend trips that Suk Hing witnessed a sight that would haunt her for a long time to come. Walking to the doctor's one day to make her mother's regular appointment, Suk Hing decided she would take a different route through the city, just for a change of scenery and to break the drudgery of the routine. The new route took her past the train station, which was quite close to her old home. As she approached the station, she noticed a large group of government soldiers. Curious, Suk Hing moved closer, crossing the street in the hopes of getting a better look. She soon wished she hadn't.

When she got a clear view, she felt sick to her stomach. The soldiers were busy piling dead bodies on top of one another and onto the back of a military vehicle. The bodies looked emaciated, their ragged clothing hung loosely around their frames, pooling in their sunken abdomens, the outline of their ribcages clear. Their skin was stretched over the bones of their hands, making them look skeletal, and their faces were grey and gaunt. Suk Hing watched in horror as the soldiers roughly manipulated the snarl of rigid limbs to fit into the back of the truck. She caught the empty gaze of one of the corpses, its slackened jaw lolling as if still in the midst of some terrible final elocution, her own body frozen as if waiting to receive this unspeakable message. As the soldiers threw the body on top of the pile, the spell was broken and Suk Hing knew she had to move along before the guards were alerted to her presence. Averting her eyes, Suk Hing made her way past the truck, pretending to see nothing of the activity beside her. She decided never to take that route again.

One weekend, in order to mitigate the loneliness and sadness of the empty house for a short while, Suk Hing made the cross-town trip to visit one of her sisters. She knew she would be welcomed, but was surprised to be greeted enthusiastically by a stranger who seemed to know her instantly.

"Oh my goodness! Suk Hing, how grown up you look!"

Her sister laughed at Suk Hing's puzzled expression.

"I can see that you don't remember Mei, she used to be part of our household when we were children."

Mei nodded. "Yes, I worked for your parents and I'm lucky enough to have remained friends with your sister. I loved working there; it was a great time in my life."

"I'm sorry I don't remember you, I was so young; I don't remember a lot, apart from the day the soldiers came."

Mei's face turned grim. "That was an awful day. Let me tell you what it was like before. It was the most beautiful house, filled with artwork and expensive furniture. Every piece of wood was hand carved with the most intricate, traditional designs. I used to love to spend time polishing them to look their best. I was part of a team of eight in charge of looking after the household and it used to take us hours to carefully dust all the vases and ornamental statues, but it was never a chore, they were too beautiful. Every day, I would see something different in the designs that I had missed before."

Suk Hing nodded. "I can vaguely remember some of it, especially being told never to touch them or play with them."

"That's right! There were so many children; it was quite a task to ensure that you all stayed away from everything. It kept me on my toes, that's for sure."

The three girls laughed at the thought of Mei chasing all the children around the large house, trying to keep an eye on them all.

"I used to send you all out to the garden to play. Do you remember the gardens at all? They were stunning."

"Not really, there's nothing left of them now. I do remember the house being quite green though."

"That's right, the gardener used to have almost as much work inside as he did out, there were so many large potted plants in huge ornamental vases all over the place. He would also plant colourful and fragrant plants in the garden and when they bloomed, he would transfer them to pots and bring them inside. Oh, the house used to smell so wonderful!"

"Suk Hing, do you remember the family dinners?" her sister asked.

Suk Hing shook her head.

"There used to be about fifty of us sitting down to dinner, we needed several tables in the dining room for us all to fit!"

"Your mother always wanted all the family to eat together. She didn't believe in the younger kids eating earlier or in the kitchen. She was a traditionalist and that meant all the family gathered for meals. I used to admire her values very much," Mei added.

"Who was that man that used to hang around all the time? I used to think he was like a butler or something, but I never saw him do any work."

Suk Hing watched the glance exchanged between her sister and her friend with interest. Her sister didn't remember any man hanging around at all.

"That was the family bodyguard," said Mei, "hired to protect you all. Your father was a very important man back then."

"Wow, I never knew we had a bodyguard!"

"Mei, what happened to father? Where did he go? Why were those soldiers after him that day?"

Mei paused and looked darkly away from the two girls: "Your father had no choice. They gave him no choice. They would have arrested him, and probably killed him. At the first opportunity, he fled to Hong Kong."

The three girls passed the rest of the afternoon reminiscing. Suk Hing learned much of how her life had been. She hadn't realized that her family had lost quite so much. Suk Hing compared the home that she'd imagined but hadn't quite known—fragrant, green, a hive of life—to the progressively dilapidated house with which she was now familiar: empty, imposing, stern, defined by its absences. The house, she realized, had taken on something of her mother's features; it felt stricken, unkind in that way that only those dispossessed of their kindness can ever really know. Suk Hing could hardly believe it was the same place they'd been talking of earlier.

On Sundays, her mother would make the difficult journey to the city, spending the day cooking and cleaning for Kin Mou. She would stay overnight to attend her appointment with the doctor on Monday, and then travel back to the farm, exhausted. As much as Suk Hing felt sorry for her mother, she cherished the opportunity to spend time alone with her grandmother, where they would talk and laugh together as they carried out the chores, forgetting their troubles for as long as they could.

Suk Hing's routine continued this way for a few years. Hunger, poverty, and despair raged through the country like wildfire. People were dying of starvation daily, their bodies unable to cope with punishing labour and little food. Suk Hing heard rumours of huge military trucks dispatched each morning to collect the dead, whose bodies were piled indiscriminately on board without dignity or respect. Not so long ago, she wouldn't have believed it. The government assigned jobs to individuals with little thought to their abilities or physical condition. There was no choice but to carry out the gruelling tasks without complaint. No one dared speak out.

———————————————

When she was eleven years old, Suk Hing dreamt of her father. She saw him wearing a brown shirt, shoes and hat, the same outfit he had been wearing the last time she had seen him before he left for Hong Kong. After she awoke, Suk Hing spoke to her mother and was shocked to find that Nim Ping Kan had had the very same dream. They would both recall that surprising moment when, a few days later, they received a letter informing them of his death, which, they were told, had occurred on the very night of the shared dream.

Her mother remained stone faced as she received the news, but Suk Hing shed tears for the father she could just barely remember. The letter didn't contain any details regarding funeral arrangements. Approval to attend would never have been granted, nor would they have been allowed to bring his body home, considering he was a fugitive and a traitor.

Shortly afterward, Nim Ping Kan announced she wanted to move back to the city. Weekly travel to the clinic had been arduous, and it simply made more sense to actually live where they were constantly needing to go. However, their years on the farm meant the government had designated them as farmers and approval was denied. Nim Ping Kan compromised by agreeing to move to a small town in the nearby in Haizhu District, which had a population of around 3,000 and many surrounding farms, all of which had been recently seized by the government. It was 1958, and the newspapers had all been proclaiming the beginning of a "Great Leap Forward." The government had abolished private property and taken control of the country's farms, combining many of them into massive plots of land which required an equally massive workforce. Such policies, it was argued, would meet the increasing demands of the population through increased human, rather than machine, labour: or, in government speak, greater "cooperation" through greater "physical effort."

Suk Hing was devastated to leave the farm and her grandmother, but knew she had no choice. Not only was her mother's word law, Suk Hing also respected her mother's decisions. As they arrived in town, Suk Hing got her first glance of the house she was to live in. It was an old, two-story, grey stone and brick construction on a street with many similar looking houses. It was unappealing from outside, and inside wasn't much better. The old, musty smell of the place indicated it had been sealed and empty for some time. Suk Hing couldn't help wonder what had happened to the people who used to live there. She assumed that the house had been seized, just as hers had, as it carried the same air of sadness and neglect. The red clay ceramic floors were dusty and cracked, and the walls were bare. Just off the long central corridor was a large, barren room, presumably once a family room. Suk Hing wondered how they were ever going to fill such a room with furniture when they could barely afford to eat.

At the end of the corridor, there were three small stone steps that led into a large bedroom with a wooden floor. A second bedroom was behind the first, a much smaller room, equally empty and neglected.

Suk Hing and her mother set about cleaning their new home. Suk Hing scrubbed and washed as hard as she could, hoping to cleanse the ghosts of other lives still lingering within. After cleaning, they needed to find an appropriate place to hang a portrait of Mao. This was non-negotiable, and since nobody had money for frivolities, Suk Hing and her mother were ordered to pick up one of the cheap, mass-produced posters from the government offices, where they were given away for free. Though it was required that Mao's "benevolent" visage be visible in the main room of the home, Nim Ping Kan put it up to the left of the bedroom door in the back of the room, nearly out of sight. This small act of defiance from her traditionalist mother surprised Suk Hing.

Their next task was to use the money they had left to buy a small clay stove, which would provide them with both heat and cooking facilities, along with a few utensils. There was no proper kitchen in the house, so Nim Ping Kan constructed a makeshift base out of some old bricks she had managed to find. She built it up on the right hand side of the main room and placed the new stove there.

Suk Hing tried to make the most of small town life. The people in the town were pleasant and easy-going, despite the hardships they faced, and Suk Hing's journey to school was far shorter, and easier. There was little consolation, though, for having lost the affection, laughter, and happiness she had experienced with her grandmother.

One of the new realities that Suk Hing did find difficult to get used to were the speakers positioned all over town, hanging mostly from trees. From the early hours of the morning, and at random periods throughout the day, the speakers would start piping out an inanely cheery voice reading various prerecorded messages extolling the wonders of their great leader and how good life was under his rule. Not only did the haphazard spew and whine of feedback grate on Suk Hing's nerves, the messages themselves, whose simpering buoyancy clashed vividly with her daily experience, filled her with frustration and anger. She attempted to block the messages out completely, but hard as she tried, the sheer repetition and volume of them meant that something always managed to filter through. She gathered that this was the whole point of them.

Soon after the move to Haizu District, the government issued strange orders. After regular working hours were over, everyone was to return to their homes and collect everything they owned that was made of metal. Government officials would be moving house to house to collect these items, and to confiscate any similar objects as they saw fit.

Suk Hing's mother was waiting for her when she returned from school, a small pile of pots, utensils and trinkets piled on the table,

"Suk Hing, help me get the rest of our cooking things on the table. Someone from the government will be here soon to pick them up"

"But why, mother? We need these things for cooking!"

"I don't know, Suk Hing. Who knows what they are up to next? Still, we have to forfeit them because we have been ordered to do so."

Suk Hing looked around the tiny kitchen area, taking stock of the few things they had left – a few clay pots, chopsticks, some eating bowls. "Can't we at least keep one cooking pot?"

"No, we can't. What if they search houses to make sure everyone followed orders? It's too risky."

Suk Hing shrugged and helped her mother gather the items.

In time, officials arrived to seize the gathered odds and ends. Suk Hing remained only dimly aware of the government's plans, though they permeated the edges of her every day life and, sometimes literally, the very air she breathed. On her daily walks to school, Suk Hing more than once noticed queues of workers hauling carts laden with a variety of household bric-a-brac — woks, doorknobs, cutlery, bicycles — towards some undisclosed locality spewing billows of smoke, like votaries on a pilgrimage to appease some new and strangely capricious household deity. She saw the local forests receding around her, and in a shockingly brief span of time, disappear almost entirely. A large number of houses were bulldozed to make way for yet more farmland. Because individuals weren't allowed to speak out against the government or ask any questions, Suk Hing never did find out what happened to the people who lost their homes. She wished she knew what had become of them, if only to know they were all right.

Soon, it was announced that food rations were no longer going to be distributed and cooked at home. The government demanded that everyone now gather for their meals in a community building, eating food prepared for them at long tables. Suk Hing couldn't really fathom the point of this new order but, as usual, she had no choice but to go along with it.

For the first four months or so the meals were actually palatable and satisfying. Along with the vegetables and rice, there was usually fish or pork, and the people of the town were allowed to go back for more, eating until they were full. It wouldn't last.

The food began to change. Meat disappeared from the menu, then fish. Soon, all that was served was rice and vegetables, but the people were pacified by the fact that they could still eat until they were full. The rest of the year carried on that way, and the people grew used to this new way of life. If anyone felt discontent with the way things were, they kept it to themselves, as always.

Chapter Three

"The starving can't choose their meals"

1959 – 1962

By 1959, conditions had worsened. The fine growing weather of the previous year was followed by a
pitiless draught.

Vegetables were no longer served during communal
meals. Rice was the only thing still on the menu, but even
that was mixed with bland taro root to add bulk and make
the grains go further. Quantities too were now rationed
and the people in the town could no longer eat as much
as they wanted. They were only allowed a small portion
and it never seemed to be enough. People were once again
going hungry.

The government came up with new plans to counteract the food shortage in the country. Suk Hing was still young and not involved in farming, but the propaganda at school was constantly informing her of the new ways the people were to be looked after, making their leaders sound like geniuses who could solve any problem. As she grew older and understood more, Suk Hing shed any doubt about the stories she had heard and began to despise the government for its arrogance. Yet she would never dare give voice to these thoughts. Outwardly, it was necessary to maintain the facade of obedience and acceptance in order to avoid punishment, whether prison or something worse. Rumours circulated about disappearances. With her own father's exodus, Suk Hing had witnessed first hand what could happen to those the government deemed undesirable. Any resistance to the education system's attempts to force her to admire the brutality of the new regime would, and must, remain carefully hidden.

The official announcement was made just before the beginning of the new rice-planting season. The government's idea was to plant double the amount of grain into the same amount of land. Bemused, Suk Hing listened as her teacher explained that instead of the eight-inch spacing between rice plants they had always used, planters would now use only four inches. It occurred to Suk Hing that if rice planters had always used eight inches, then surely that was the space needed for the plants to grow properly. The farmers couldn't have been wrong all those years about how best to grow their crops.

It was also announced that sweet potato was to be grown differently, namely by planting them deeper into the ground and in a different orientation. Suk Hing's suspicions were confirmed when she later overheard a group farmers in town whispering that this was a bad idea and wasn't going to work. No one dared to question the new rules but it was obvious that the people had no faith in the plans that were being imposed upon them.

As the year progressed, the situation grew steadily worse. The new planting methods were failing; crops were not developing in the way that they should have been. Meals were rationed at only three ounces of cooked rice per meal in order to preserve the supplies they already had. Suk Hing could measure the food on her plate as being two fingers wide and two fingers long of her small hand.

The farmers were ordered to dig trenches alongside the rice paddy fields with the suggestion that it would allow more oxygen to circulate around the crops. They followed every instruction the government threw at them, but all the ideas were ineffective and it was looking like that year's crops were going to fail. The meals that were served were now just a watered-down rice porridge, an unappetizing slop that held little nutritional value. The propaganda continued, with the government informing people not to be concerned, a solution would be found as long as everyone worked together and obeyed the rules.

Over the next two years the situation grew more desperate. It was now 1961, and most of the people pulled away from farming had been sent away to work on building a large-scale irrigation system outside of town. Suk Hing was still in school and for this she was glad. The work was a two-hour walk away from the township, and rather than make the journey day in day out, the people were required to stay close to the project. Most of them were gone for months at a time and the town was practically deserted.

With no one to tend to them, the crops lay abandoned and rotting in the fields. The irrigation system was a long way from finished and the new crops that it would hopefully bring about were a long time in the future; yet the food shortage was immediate and required a quick resolution as well as a long-term plan. The answer to the short term problems should have been to salvage what was left of the season's pitiful crops. It might not have solved the problem entirely, but it certainly would have helped.

The food shortage had now become drastic. The lack of nutrition in the meals provided by the government over the last two years meant that many of the town's elderly had perished. Babies were sickly due to the poor quality of their mother's milk, and even many of the strongest men were now becoming too malnourished to work.

Suk Hing couldn't believe what was happening around her. The government's idea of a redistribution of wealth had, instead, brought the country to its knees, with no wealth for anyone, save those already within the government and the military. How could they not see that there wouldn't be a country left? That there wouldn't be any surviving people to rule over if they didn't rethink their strategies?

The government eventually gave up on the idea of communal eating; once again, people returned to cooking food in their own homes. Food was still rationed, however, and each of them were still only allowed three ounces of rice per meal.

Finally, when everyone was starving and sick, the irrigation system was complete. Planting reverted back to the old methods and everyone pinned their hopes on the new crops to save them in time.

All through these lean and terrible years, the speakers continued to blare incongruous, cheery messages: "Study Chairman Mao's writing!"

"Follow his teachings and act according to his instruction!"

Suk Hing scoffed at the continual announcements which they had no choice but to follow.

Chapter Four

"If one does not plow, there will be no harvest."

1962 – 1966

Suk Hing's formal education ended after her fifteenth birthday. Sixteen was the oldest the government allowed anyone to stay in school, putting them to work as soon as they reached this age, no matter how much aptitude they showed for education. The government didn't want men and women educated to the point where they might think for themselves: they wanted workers.

For all that, staying at school for another few months seemed pointless to Suk Hing. Her family desperately needed money. It was 1962, and despite the changes made, the situation was too far gone to see much improvement. As Suk Hing matured, she learned more of how the government used fear and poverty to control the people. She also learned that it had become virtually impossible for anyone to really earn a decent living; the government kept wages low and capped everyone's earnings at measly amounts.

Kin Mou had returned from the city, giving the family another mouth to feed. The government ordered him to sign up as a farmer the same as his sister. Sitting with Suk Hing in the bland, under-furnished house, Kin Mou waited until Nim Ping Kan retired for the night before broaching a difficult subject.

"Suk Hing, can you keep a secret?"

"Of course, brother," she replied, curious. They had been apart for so long that Suk Hing didn't exactly consider them close, and she was surprised her brother wished to confide in her with something that sounded so serious.

"I don't want to stay here and I don't want to farm. I am tired of the regime, tired of the poverty, starvation and death I see every day."

Suk Hing was startled. Although she felt the same way, no one ever dared speak out against the government. She wondered if it was a trick; if someone had spotted her contempt and disbelief in the propaganda that had been served up to her at school. *Perhaps her brother was trying to get her to admit her distaste for the government, and then the soldiers would come and arrest her.* Not quite trusting the situation, she remained silent, gesturing with her hand for her brother to continue.

"There are no opportunities. I spent all that time at school, and for what? To labour in the fields of the state-run farms, earning a pittance, and receiving a certificate giving me the right to buy food? Why should any government be allowed that much power, to decide who is allowed to buy food and who isn't?"

"But what else can you do?" she asked, fearful of the consequences of his impassioned speech. "Think of the outcome if you refuse."

"I have already refused."

Suk Hing gasped; she was shocked to hear that a member of her own family had taken such a stand against the system that ruled their lives.

"What happened?" she asked in almost a whisper, as if afraid of the question as well as the answer.

"They laughed, and said I would soon change my mind once I was starving."

Kin Mou removed his food certificate from his pocket to show her. Suk Hing stared glumly at the large red letters stamped across the certificate: "DENIED." There wasn't a single place in China that Kin Mou could legally buy food.

"What are we going to do?" she asked sadly, knowing that they would now have to stretch their daily ration of three ounces of rice to accommodate him. They couldn't let him starve, but they would all have a little less now.

"Don't worry; I won't be a burden for long. I'm going to Hong Kong where people have a chance, where they can work and earn a fair wage, enough to live, not barely exist."

Suk Hing knew enough to know that the island was under British rule, exempt from the harsh communist regime of mainland China. Despite her dislike of the political situation, she had never taken the time to consider the implications of the different situation in Hong Kong.

Hearing her brother talk of it now, the idea both terrified and thrilled her.

"How will you get there?"

"Swim," Kin Mou replied simply.

"That's crazy!" A shudder went through Suk Hing as she thought of the dangers, the gruelling journey and the risk of capture.

"You'll never make it. You'll be caught and sent to jail, shot, or drown. Please reconsider?"

Her brother shook his head. "My mind is made up. Besides, Dad made it and so did Li; he's there now, waiting for me to join him." Kin Mou grinned at his sister's shocked face. If the government found out the family were in touch with their eldest brother, who was now considered a traitor, they would all be severely punished, probably by a prison sentence at best.

"How did he get there? How do you know he's alive?"

"Do you remember Chang Chang?"

"Your old school friend? We met a few times."

"Best you don't know too much, little sister, but she and her family have connections. They all make a living from helping escapees, so can set up safe houses along the way on quite a few of the popular routes. I'll ask her to set some up for me, the same as she did for Li. Now, don't ask any more and promise me you will never speak of this conversation again," he said as he rose to retire, ruffling her cropped, jet-black hair.

She watched his retreating back for a second before blurting out, "I'm coming with you!"

Her brother turned and looked at her sadly.

"You're too young and too delicate. Look at yourself, Suk Hing; you'd never make it. Anyway, you need to stay and look after mother. I'm sorry, little sister, but your place is here by her side."

Suk Hing hung her head, knowing her brother spoke the truth, but resenting the implications that she was too weak to make it.

●————————————————————————●

Suk Hing arose at five a.m. the next morning to complete a few household chores and prepare a meagre breakfast for her family. At six, she left the house and joined the working population of China for the first time.

Others were already in the street, making small talk in the cool morning air as they made their way to the town square. Among the steadily growing crowd Suk Hing noticed her friend Jin Jing who, being slightly older, had already been pulled from school and sent to work in the fields.

As they walked together, Suk Hing tried to discern what she could about what was in store for her.

"What happens when we get to the town square?"

"There's a chalkboard there with all the different farms and plantations in the area listed on it. Our names are written next to the place we are to work today. Soldiers with huge guns guard the board to ensure it isn't tampered with, and to make sure we all head in the right direction without complaint."

As they walked, Jin Jing had to raise her voice to be heard over the speakers, which were concentrated in the town centre. Suk Hing reluctantly listened to the first message of many that day.

"Comrade Mao Zedong is the greatest Marxist-Leninist of our era. He has inherited, defended, and developed Marxism–Leninism with genius, both creatively and comprehensively, and has brought it to a higher and completely new stage."

On arrival in the town square, Suk Hing was shocked to see the reality of the situation before her, belying everything she had just heard.

The people that gathered in the square beside her were not well fed and cared for by their new administration and supposed employment. Forced to become peasant farmers, everyone appeared thin and sickly, some almost skeletal, bones sticking out from every part of their body, their cheeks sunken and their eyes circled with dark rings.

The propaganda made the state farms and jobs sound like a wonderful idea. They stated that no one should be entitled to hold too much personal wealth while others went without, claiming that their seizure and redistribution programs would benefit everyone. It was clear from what she had seen that morning that those who had been poor before the Communist take over seemed no better off, and those who had been wealthy were struggling with the continual hours of forced hard labor. Away from the isolation of her grandmother's home, Suk Hing was even more convinced that the government were fools and liars.

It was a pitiful sight, and Suk Hing now had firsthand experience of the flawed ideology that her teachers had tried to drum into her with so much passion in school. The only ones who looked strong and healthy were the soldiers that continually watched the townspeople. It was obvious that whatever had been seized and whatever was being produced was going in that direction first, ensuring that the government and all its employees were getting the lion's share of everything, while the rest were left to suffer and struggle.

No matter what people had been in their former lives, they were all equal now in the soldiers' eyes. Equal not as citizens, but as common, peasant "scum," nothing more than animals to be worked as hard as they could be until they died from exhaustion and starvation. Suk Hing could read it in their mocking and sneering faces and averted gazes, and in the downtrodden manner of the people awaiting their chance to see where they were required to head to that day.

Jin Jing pushed her way to the board. She searched for both their names, and then returned to Suk Hing's side with a smile on her face, her cheerfulness a great comfort in the midst of such misery.

"Great news, we're working at the same place today, so I can show you the ropes. Come on, we'd best get a move on. If we're late by even a minute one whole hour gets deducted from our wages."

"Where are we working?" Suk Hing panted as her friend grasped her arm and pulled her along at a rapid pace, rushing to their employment for the day along with the rest of the group.

"The paddy fields at the southern outskirts of town. Now come on! There's no time to dawdle."

"Look at these people, half of them don't look fit to do a day's work," Suk Hing hissed to her friend as they walked.

"They don't have a lot of choice, do they?" Jin Jing replied quietly.

"What happens if they get really sick and can't work?"

"The government has its own way of dealing with them. Suk Hing, we shouldn't be talking about this."

"Tell me," she demanded. She knew that the hardship she had suffered in her earlier life was nothing compared to what she faced now. She needed to fully understand the situation. She had read between the lines and seen through the propaganda she had been forced to swallow at school, but now she wanted facts, the absolute truth underneath the pretty picture the government tried so hard to paint.

"If someone gets really sick, they find an excuse to revoke their food certificate, some invented offence against the government. They soon die."

Suk Hing's hand flew to cover her mouth in shock. "That's horrible!"

Jin Jing shrugged. "It's the way things are now. It saves them being a drain on resources, a quick and easy way to get rid of them so that the rations can go to people still able to carry out their duties. It also means that they don't cost the government money in healthcare. Look at us all, do you really think we have a choice in the matter? We're not exactly strong enough to hold an uprising and fight, are we?"

"I can't believe this."

"You will, the first time someone takes ill or dies in the field right beside you. When you see them hauled away and laid in a pile for the wagons to pick up, lying there like nothing more than an empty sack, thrown onto the wagon in heaps like rotten animal carcasses, you'll believe it all then."

"Does that happen a lot?"

"All the time. The wagon makes its rounds of all the farms and the town on a daily basis to take away the dead."

"This is awful; there must be something we can do."

"I wish there was, but we are just two girls, what can we do? Now please, Suk Hing, stop asking me questions about this. I feel as badly as you do, but we are powerless, and talking about it will only get us into trouble."

Suk Hing glanced around her. "There aren't any soldiers close by; they're at the front and back of the group."

Jin Jing shook her head. "You have so much to learn, my friend. Thinking that way is going to land you in jail, or publicly beaten as an example. It's not just the soldiers that are a danger to you. Anyone listening to us could run to the nearest soldier and report our conversation."

"Why would people do that? Surely we should stick together?"

"You would think so, but that isn't how it works, at least not anymore. You'll understand it better once you have been doing this for a while. The work is tremendously hard, the pay is diabolical, and the rations are never enough. Extreme poverty and hunger does strange things to people, Suk Hing; out here it is every man and woman for themselves. People will lie, cheat, bargain, plead, steal, anything they can to survive. It's as if we have been left only with the basic instinct to stay alive, whatever that takes. If someone thinks they have something or some knowledge that will ingratiate them with the soldiers, even for a little while, they are going to use it to their best advantage."

"There have to be some good people left," Suk Hing muttered, trying to take in every terrible fact she had learned on her very first morning as a member of the working population.

"There probably are, but finding them isn't easy. Remember: you can trust no one, not even your own family or closest friend. These are the times we live in now. You might as well get used to it, put a smile on your face, and deal with it. Whatever you feel inside, keep it there and get on with what you are required to do. Don't make trouble, Suk Hing; nothing good can ever come from attracting attention to yourself. I'm begging you; let's change the subject as I don't want to get beaten to a bloody pulp and spend the night in a jail cell for being an agitator."

The girls carried out the rest of their journey in silence, Suk Hing in quiet contemplation, and Jin Jing relieved that her friend had stopped raising taboo subjects. It was a long walk but they finally arrived at the rice farm, where they had to stand in line to each be given a field number and the equipment they would need for the work. As farmers were moved around from job to job, never in steady employment, they didn't own the things they needed to work in the various fields and relied on the overseers of the farms to provide them. This was mostly done in silence, or as few words as possible, but Jin Jing shocked Suk Hing by stepping out of line to approach the farm manager and ask if she could stay close to Suk Hing that day, as she was new and would need instruction. The manager shrugged, swapping Suk Hing's number with another worker. It saved him the time and effort of assigning someone to show the tiny new girl the ropes.

The girls got back in line together and were each handed a large, heavy sickle and bales of thick twine. The equipment was old and not in the best condition, but the sickles were kept very sharp. Jin Jing warned Suk Hing to be careful as they made their way to their assigned field, where the girls were positioned by another manager at the beginning of a row. Following Jin Jing's lead, Suk Hing removed her shoes. The deep water needed to grow the rice had been drained, and the muddy soil that remained squelched between Suk Hing's toes as she took her first step onto the field. Some people were wearing thick-soled sandals held onto their feet by a single piece of fabric across the middle of their foot. Suk Hing stared at the sandals longingly as the cold, wet mud clung to the soles of her feet. The plants, too, were very wet, and Suk Hing soon found herself soaked through as she stooped to work amongst them, cutting the plants low down with the sickle. She struggled with the sweeping motion required to cut a decent amount, finding the knife strange and unwieldy in her small, inexperienced hands. After a few hours' practice and constant advice from Jin Jing, Suk Hing eventually became accustomed with the awkward motion, and was able to keep up, cutting decent-sized bundles, tying them up with thick string, and laying them down to be collected behind her.

The shift seemed to last forever. By the end, Suk Hing's back ached from stooping, her arms throbbed from the weight of the sickle, and her hands were cracked and raw from handling the wet plants. All through the day she had been plagued by the giant mosquitos that thrived in the damp environment. Angry red bite marks covered her body, and the sharp plants had left cuts and abrasions over her hands, arms, and legs. She coughed violently as she walked with Jin Jing to hand in her equipment, and was surprised by the pain that shot through in her chest. She had always been healthy, and this sudden struggle to breathe came as a nasty shock.

"That's the dust mites and mold spores that live in the plants," her friend explained. "If you can afford sandals and a mask, you'd be much better off."

Suk Hing shook her head, knowing those were luxuries her family could never afford. Her friend nodded understandingly and dropped the subject, returning to her teaching.

"Our first shift finishes at one p.m. Then we have a break before we need to return to the board and see where we have to work for the rest of the afternoon. I don't have much lunch to eat so it doesn't take long. You need to wash those cuts. There are parasites that thrive in the wet fields, and you have to be very careful to avoid infection. They can kill you if you're not strong enough to fight them off, but we're young and healthy and have the best chance. It doesn't hurt to take precautions, though, as you know now what happens if you get too sick to work."

"How long do we have for our lunch break?" Suk Hing asked, glossing over her friend's allusion to their earlier conversation. She needed some quiet time to think that over and come to terms with it before she spoke of it again.

"Our next shift begins at two-thirty p.m., so we have to get back to the board by two at the latest, as we don't know how far we'll have to walk to the next place. Let's find a place to wash and eat lunch. Did you bring anything?" Jin Jing asked, looking at Suk Hing's lack of pockets.

The morning's labour had made Suk Hing ravenous. Hunger gnawed at her insides, but she had a feeling it was a sensation she was going to have to get used to. "I thought … I thought perhaps our employers would feed us."

Jin Jing laughed at her friend's naivety. "As if anyone has food to spare like that! I'll share today, but make sure you bring your own with you tomorrow."

After finding a place to wash their wounds, the two girls sat on the ground, resting their aches and pains and drying off their wet clothes. Jin Jing plunged into the deep folds of her ankle-length skirt and victoriously revealed a minuscule sandwich, breaking off half and handing it to Suk Hing. Suk Hing looked at the morsel and instantly felt guilty.

"Are you sure?"

"Go on, eat it. I can't have you passing out on me this afternoon, can I?"

Suk Hing gratefully accepted and swallowed the food in one small bite. It barely made a dent in the hunger pangs she was experiencing, but she was very grateful to her friend for sharing what she had. It proved that her earlier suspicions had been right; there were some good people left in this world. No matter what circumstances they were forced to endure some would always retain a level of human decency and empathy. Despite everything else she had lost, she desperately wanted to hold on to those.

After their slight lunch, the girls rose stiffly to their feet and headed back to the chalkboard in the town square to receive their next assignment of the day.

"Yes!" Jin Jing shouted gleefully. "We're picking peaches this afternoon!"

"Why is that so good?" Suk Hing asked, slightly confused. Picking fruit wasn't exactly the pastime of her dreams.

"You have no idea how good it feels to stretch out your back in the afternoon after stooping all morning. Not to mention the earth is dry and so are the plants. It's still very hard work, especially carrying the full baskets and climbing for the higher fruit, but at least you don't get soaked through. Other than falling, insect stings are the worst hazard, so it's much better than working in the rice fields."

"In other words, you're telling me that we have to be grateful for small mercies"

"Exactly!"

The girls laughed as they headed to the next farm. This day was hard on Suk Hing, but having her friend by her side made coping easier.

The girls stayed close for the rest of the afternoon and chattered as they worked, which helped pass the time. They were closely watched, but as long as their hands moved as quickly as their tongues, they wouldn't be reprimanded.

Suk Hing learned that, she would earn around 75 yuan per year. She wondered how in the world she and her family would survive on this paltry sum, and what else she could possibly do but grin and bear it. The others had to, so she knew she had no choice, but still, the meagre pay shocked her.

At the end of that first day, Suk Hing ached all over. She felt muscles in places she didn't know muscles existed; and all of them throbbed and burned.

"I'll be so glad to get home."

"Oh, you can't go home yet," Jin Jing informed her. "We have to attend the meeting."

Suk Hing groaned. "What meeting?"

"You're a member of the working population now; government meetings after work are obligatory for all of us. Don't worry, you don't have to contribute, just stand and look like you are listening, and cheer and applaud in all the right places."

Dispirited, Suk Hing followed Jin Jing to the meeting point, where they, along with the rest of town, were forced to endure an hour of speeches either standing or sitting on the ground. The meetings were a more intense variant of the propaganda she had heard in school. Suk Hing considered these little more than brainwashing, an attempt to force communist notions upon the people, thus ensuring they accepted them and didn't revolt. She had to be careful not to let her expression give away the anger she felt at the by now too familiar rhetoric extolling the virtues of labour that were directed at the poor, miserable people around her, people whose only desire was go home and rest their aching bodies.

Alternately standing and sitting through the hour-long speeches had further stiffened Suk Hing's own throbbing muscles. Her body screamed as she attempted to get it moving again for the long walk home. Closing her eyes to shut out the pain, she forced herself on, eventually arriving back at the dreary house to carry out the rest of her chores. Only then, could she finally rest.

Over time, Suk Hing learned to endure the gruelling hours of manual labor she was subjected to each and every day. She discovered that picking sugar cane was by far the worst of the jobs available to those in the town forced to be farmers. The plants grew tall, some up to ten-feet-high. Tough and thick, the cane's integument had to be trimmed with care and precision close to the ground using a machete-style knife. The shoots themselves had edges like saws, which cut her small body all over. The cut stalks then had to be tied into long, heavy, bundles and carefully placed for the collectors. Working so low to the ground for hours at a time was backbreaking. To straighten up for any length of time was to stop working, catching the attention of the unforgiving supervisors that oversaw the harvest. The result was a verbal, or physical, reminder to get back to work.

She also learned to keep a placid expression on her face during the nightly meetings, hiding her contempt for the government. It was the one thing she longed to discuss, but could never take the risk. She had come to know many people in the town, making friends with those who gathered at the chalkboard in the early hours of the morning. The workers passed the time with each other on the jobs where it was permitted or possible, and Suk Hing hadn't come across anyone with whom she couldn't get along whilst working alongside them. The people remained friendly and pleasant in the face of adversity, at least on the surface.

There was hardly any time for socializing outside working hours. Initially, she was too exhausted and had too much to do at home. She never heard anyone express as much as slight disillusionment with the people in charge. To be overheard by the wrong person would mean imprisonment, corporeal punishment, perhaps even death. To speak out was to be branded a traitor, which carried the harshest penalties. Nobody would risk it where there might be government sympathizers in their midst. Suk Hing couldn't talk to her family about it either; they could easily be punished if they were suspected of knowing how she truly felt. With no chance to express her feelings, either at work or at home, they festered inside her and grew more powerful.

Just after Suk Hing turned sixteen, her brother Kin Mou disappeared. She knew from their earlier, secret conversation that he must have made his escape attempt. She awaited news of his whereabouts with both fear and trepidation. She wanted to hear that he had made it, for the idea gave her hope

for the future, but she was also afraid to receive word from him under the watchful eye of the soldiers. Correspondence with a traitor was strictly forbidden and carried stiff penalties for all members of a family if any were caught in the act.
She was devastated when she finally heard whispers that Kin Mou had been captured en route and was now imprisoned with no visitation rights. She was desperate to talk to him, to learn of his attempt and ensure he was all right. She never had the opportunity, as on his release he was ordered to work on a commune, far from the family home. He had been forced to become just another peasant farmer on a state-run farm like the government had wanted him to be all along, except now he was also branded a traitor.

The harvest was nearly over and farm work was beginning to slow. In an effort to supplement the family income, Suk Hing managed to find a job at a swimming pool. Suk Hing was pleasantly surprised to learn that she was free to use the pool after her shift for free. Swimming at once kept Suk Hing's body supple and eased the terrible aches and pains caused by the long hours of labouring in awkward positions. She began to feel healthier, though the constant, gnawing hunger remained.

One night, she looked at her small frame in the mirror in her bedroom. Her brother's words echoed in her mind: *"You're too small, you'd never make it."* Although malnourishment kept Suk Hing small and slender, she had nevertheless developed muscles in her arms and legs, and her body was toned. Under the circumstances she was in the best shape she could possibly hope to achieve. The breath of an idea began to form in her mind. Initially, she pushed it aside, ignoring the small murmur, but it gradually became a voice, then a shout, inside her head.

She began listening to the voice, taking it more seriously, giving it due thought and consideration. She stepped up her swimming regime despite the exhaustion and the constant work and chores.

By the time she was eighteen, Suk Hing had come to a final decision. The country was showing no signs of improvement, the government holding hard and fast to their ideological commitments, and the people too afraid to question or stand against them. She needed to get away. She had to attempt the journey to Hong Kong. She risked capture, or even death in the endeavour, but it had to be worth the risk. There was nothing for her here anymore, except years of labour leading to an early grave from malnutrition and starvation.

That night, Suk Hing dreamt of her brother. In the dream, Kin Mou stood at the edge of her bed and in the darkness he repeated his final admonition: *you'd never make it.* The words sent a chill through Suk Hing's entire body.

"I'm not making it here, Kin Mou. No one is."

"Do you really think you'll succeed where I failed?"

"I don't know. I have to try."

Kin Mou smiled, and repeated something half forgotten from their childhood:

"There is a book called Qi Xie, a record of marvels. We have in it these words. 'In the Northern Ocean there is a fish, the name of which is Kun. . . It changes into a bird with the name of Peng. When this bird rouses itself and flies, its wings are like clouds all round the sky. When the

sea is moved so as to bear it along, it prepares to remove to the Southern Ocean. The Southern Ocean is the Pool of Heaven.'"

By morning, Suk Hing had decided to leave.

Chapter Five

"A journey of a 1000 miles starts beneath one's feet."

February 1ˢᵗ, 1966

Now that Suk Hing had decided to escape, she felt a great weight lifted from her shoulders. The only problem was that she actually had no idea where to begin. She needed to work on an actual plan, and then find the courage to execute it. She knew that the longer she waited, the harder it would be to go. Taking the only option she felt she had, she confided in Jin Jing. Jin Jing had lived in the town much longer than Suk Hing and might have heard a lot more about those who had already attempted the journey to Hong Kong. Jin Jing seemed knowledgeable about so many things, Suk Hing was certain she would have information. She might even know how people started off and whether they made it. Asking was a huge risk, for both Suk Hing and Jin Jing, but at least Suk Hing knew she could trust her friend.

That night after the meeting, Suk Hing asked Jin Jing to accompany her for a walk in the local park. The park was the main community area of the town, with a small plot of grass and a few scattered benches. Hundreds of people gathered there each day to chat and relax after the long work hours were over; it was their only time to socialize in peace. Suk Hing gently guided her friend to a quiet area away from others who might overhear. It was now or never.

"I need to speak with you," she murmured in a low voice, close to her friend's ear.

"Oh, Suk Hing, we've been together all day, you could have spoken to me any time," her closest friend laughed.

"No, this needs to be in private, so no one can overhear, and you must promise me your secrecy. Do you promise not to breathe a word of what I say to anyone?"

"Of course, Suk Hing! What is this about? Tell me quickly, you're beginning to frighten me."

"I'm going to try and get to Hong Kong."

Her friend's eyes grew wide and she grabbed Suk Hing's arm, linking it with her own so she could pull her close and hiss in her ear.

"Are you crazy? Where is this coming from? You haven't said a word or made any sign that you don't agree with the government. What's brought this about?"

The two girls plastered smiles on their faces as they walked arm in arm, just two friends out for a stroll, talking of things of no consequence to anyone but each other.

"I've felt this way ever since I was old enough to understand what the government stood for. There is nothing here for me, except you of course, but I have to go. The only problem is I don't know where to start. I don't suppose you have any connections, or have heard how others have done it?"

Jin Jing hesitated before she decided to answer her friend honestly. "Yes, actually I do. I have a friend who has a friend who knows some things. Let's sit down on the grass here and I'll tell you what I can."

Suk Hing listened carefully as Jin Jing talked, filing every scrap of information away for future consideration.

"Hundreds try each day, from all over the mainland. The more that try, the more the escape points become known to the soldiers, and the tighter the security gets. Guard towers have been hastily erected over many of the shorelines up and down the coast. Hong Kong still has its borders open but there are rumours that they won't be for much longer. They fear the city's going to become over populated, and they're going to have to limit the amount of refugees they take. It's said that it'll become just as dangerous to be caught at the other end as it is being caught at this end."

"How long have you known about all this?" Suk Hing asked, fascinated by her friend's knowledge.

Jin Jing shrugged, "Awhile, but I never knew you were interested or felt the way you did. It's not something you casually bring up in conversation."

"What do you know of the actual journey?"

"Vague details, I know it's a long journey to get to a crossing point that's even remotely passable. I've heard the distance from Guangzhou is close to 100 kilometres, but that's not counting the out of the way routes you'd need to use to avoid detection. *And* there's the long swim across the Zhujiang River. In the dark. Lots of people don't make it, Suk Hing. Just as many get caught before they even make it as far as the water, or die of starvation during the journey itself. Are you certain about doing this?"

"I've never been more certain of anything in my life. I have to do this."

Jin Jing looked resigned and sad, but nodded. "Fine, give me a couple of days to talk to my friend, and we'll take it from there. Come on, we'd best get home or our families will start to worry, and we both still have chores to do."

Over the next few weeks, the girls made a habit of strolling in the park together, unnoticed and not raising any suspicion amongst the hundreds of others who gathered there. Jin Jing had told Suk Hing of a few people who would have more information. They had a rough description, but nothing else to go on. As they made their way among the people that gathered in the park daily, they kept an eye out for anyone who might fit the bill.

Suk Hing also started smuggling away a few tiny grains of rice wherever she could. She couldn't spare much, but thought a few grains per day would mount up. She had no idea when she might have to go, and needed to be prepared. If she couldn't take it, perhaps she could at least have a decent meal before she set off. She had no doubt she would make it happen, one way or another.

She also intensified her training at the swimming pool, trying to fit in fifty laps every single day, preparing her muscles for the strenuous journey that she hoped her future would hold. She also tried to save the odd few coins here and there, hiding them under her mattress in her room. The money was still only a pittance after several months, but it was better than nothing at all. At the very least, she felt she was doing something to make her escape a reality and not just a hopeless dream.

One fresh, early February night in 1966, Suk Hing's luck changed. Walking as usual with Jin Jing, she spotted two men who had separated themselves a little from the rest of the crowd. They were talking with their heads bent low and their eyes were on constant look out for anyone approaching them or getting too close. She nudged Jin Jing and motioned to them briefly with her head. Jin Jing studied the two men.

"They seem to fit the general description," Jin Jing agreed. "What age would you say they were?"

Age was a difficult thing to determine due to the hard lives the people were forced to endure, and Suk Hing considered carefully before answering. "My best guess would be somewhere between twenty and twenty-five."

"I think so too, so that fits; and they do seem to be sharing a secret. Do you think we should approach them?"

"Of course," Suk Hing replied. "I can't let this slip through my fingers. Perhaps you should stay here though, if we get caught, it's better that you aren't seen with us."

Jin Jing let her friend go, watching anxiously from a distance.

"Excuse me," Suk Hing said in a timid voice, approaching the two men. "I'm looking to buy a soccer ball for my brother. You look like you might play, and I was wondering if you could recommend a place to purchase one?"

Jin Jing had already told her that escapees often purchased soccer ball bladders to use as makeshift floats to aid them in the journey, something they could cling to, helping them to keep afloat if they couldn't swim anymore. They were something that could be passed off as a gift or a replacement for a burst one if questioned and they could be deflated and packed easily into a backpack, and then blown up again once the sea was within sight. Suk Hing hoped that if these were the right men, they would recognize her question as some sort of code, realizing what she really wanted without having to speak it aloud. If they weren't the men she sought, they would think her a little odd, but probably no more than that. She could turn it around to make it sound innocent if the wrong person suspected something and reported her.

The two turned in her direction and looked at her warily.

"I'm sorry, but neither of us play, we can't help you," one said, with a cold expression on his face.

"Oh, I was so certain you were the two I had been told to look for, are you sure you don't have any knowledge at all about soccer balls?"

"We don't know what you're talking about, our apologies, but we have to go."

With that, the men walked away briskly, leaving Suk Hing dejected. Jin Jing hurried to her side and led her off.

"Don't worry, it's to be expected that they would be cautious of strangers. You could be a sympathizer for the government. Let things settle then try again once they see nothing bad has happened since your approach."

There was nothing for Suk Hing to do except take her friend's advice. She carried on as normal for a few days, working, swimming, attending the meetings and strolling in the park with Jin Jing. She spotted the men again but didn't try to approach them until the fifth day. This time she was more direct, too tired of waiting to worry so much about the consequences if she were wrong.

"I want out, and I've been told you are the ones to make it happen, so are you going to help me?" she said in a low but determined voice as she marched up to them.

The two men laughed. "You're too young and small to be that feisty," they teased her.

Suk Hing all but stamped her foot with frustration. "I'm eighteen, almost nineteen, old enough to know my own mind. I may be small and thin, but isn't everyone? I'm stronger than I look; I'm a farmer and a lifeguard."

Her impassioned speech piqued their interest. "A lifeguard? So you're a good swimmer?"

"Fifty laps every day without stopping, minimum."

"Well, that does help," one of the men muttered. They exchanged a glance, seemingly communicating silently between them. They had obviously come to a silent agreement when one of them spoke.

"We might be who you are looking for," he admitted. "Meet us back here in three days' time and maybe we can talk some more."

Suk Hing was happy enough to turn cartwheels as they walked away, but she kept herself in check until she and Jin Jing had left the park. As they walked, they whispered and giggled, looking like any normal girls who had encountered a handsome suitor. It was the perfect cover and anyone who witnessed their antics smiled, pleased to see some happiness could still be found amongst the young, despite the harshness of their existence.

Suk Hing's nerves soon settled into a grim determination over the next few meetings with the two men. They were wary of her initially, careful not to reveal too much, giving very general information and making it all sound like rumour and speculation. The two men remained cryptic, unwilling to commit to imparting the hard facts that Suk Hing needed from them. She never learned their names, or where they lived. Personal information was taboo. One day, Suk Hing broke that rule, mentioning her brother by name when talking of past attempts made and routes used.

"Kin Mou?" one of the men asked. "I know Kin Mou; he came to us for help with a group of others. He became a good friend of mine, which is why I know his real name."

"Do you know if he ever got the opportunity to try again? I know he was caught the first time."

The man shook his head. "You're right. As far as I know, he is still in the commune. I am sure he will try again; my friends are keeping an eye on him and waiting for the right time to approach him. The opportunity will present itself."

From that point on, the men trusted Suk Hing, and she was let into the plan. They were to wait until June; the warmer months made the sea more bearable for the swim. A maximum of five escapees would be sent at a time, trying to keep a low profile and not attract too much attention en route. They recommended a backpack each containing one soccer ball bladder, and food and water for a week if they could manage to gather it together. They also recommended that each group carry a compass to share, or one each if they could, in case they were separated at any point in the journey.

Over the weeks, the meetings continued, with people coming and going. Sometimes there were as many as a dozen people in the group, yet as the park grew busier as the weather turned warmer, they still did not attract undue attention from the soldiers that patrolled the town day and night.

The people who came were mixed, but all shared the same hatred and fear of the government. It was a relief for Suk Hing to discover the whole country hadn't been brainwashed into believing their lies. One man was about fifty-years-old, and everyone's heart broke a little when he was informed for his own good that he would never make the journey. They all wished him well as he left, but knew his life would hold nothing but sadness.

During one of the many meetings, Suk Hing decided to question the group leaders about the bodies she had seen at the train station in the city. Not only had the visions plagued her, but also the explanation eluded her. She had tried to understand why there had been so many bodies, but it still made no sense to her.

The group leader nodded, his face sympathetic. "I'm sorry you had to see something like that at such a young age, but this is an example of what is happening all over China. In the rural areas, life is very bad. People are forced to work too hard, aren't fed enough and the soldiers are freer to treat people cruelly. Many flee to the larger cities, hoping they will be invisible there, perhaps finding jobs and places to stay. All too often, they can't find work and they end up homeless and starving. The train station is one of the few places that is open all night and they seek refuge there to sleep. What you saw that day were the ones that didn't wake up that morning."

The group gave a collective gasp of horror and Suk Hing placed a hand over her mouth. "You mean that might be the numbers on a daily basis?"

"Probably, yes."

That particular meeting was brought to a hurried end, but the shocking conversation had only served to fire their determination even more, no matter how severe the risks. All those that came to express their wish to escape were given the same grave warnings. Military checkpoints and borders were in place all over the country and every town and village was occupied by armed military personnel. Many of the routes were becoming known to the government and were more heavily guarded than they had been previously. Options were narrowing, margins for error slimming. The only routes that were still safe usually involved crossing the southern mountain ranges at some point, making it an arduous and deadly journey. They would be at the mercy of the landscape, the foot and air patrols, the elements, and the wildlife that lived up there. Most changed their minds once they heard the full dangers and low odds of survival. Suk Hing, however, did not.

Suk Hing was allocated two travelling companions and a date of June nineteenth for her departure. Suk Hing got to know her travelling companions, who were both young men about the same age as the leaders of the group. They were pleasant and friendly, and Suk Hing felt she was lucky to be assigned to their group. One was outgoing and fearless, while the other was more reserved and slightly more worried about the experience to come. Although she never knew their names, she felt that she knew their personalities well, and that the three of them had already bonded. The wait would be tense, but the careful planning and memorizing of their specific route helped to pass the time, as did the squirrelling away of the few coins and food that she could spare. Settling upon a route would be difficult. Many of the most obvious ways were now used so frequently that they were heavily guarded and watched. The leaders of the group helped them, pointing out the methods of transport that they should avoid at all costs due to so many being captured whilst using them. The main ferry from Guangzhou was out of the question, but there were other options, smaller ferries with more infrequent routes. The three finally agreed upon a route that added time, but gave them a better chance.

Two months after she was fully included in the meetings, Suk Hing decided she needed to be more proactive. The more they spoke of the journey, the more dangerous she realized it was going to be. She would be at risk of being identified as a runaway at many points as they had to use public transport. There was no doubt that the journey would be taxing as well as risky, with hours and hours of walking and mountainous terrain to cross. She recalled her brother's mentioning his old school friend, Chang Chang, before he made his own escape attempt. Given Kin Mou's fate, visiting Chang Chang would pose significant risk. Suk Hing wasn't even sure if the woman would help. Perhaps her brother had been mistaken about Chang Chang's contacts, or her knowledge of any safe houses or routes to the coast. Perhaps Chang Chang had been discovered as an ally to the freedom swimmers and was now under arrest or being carefully watched. Though uncertain, Suk Hing decided to make the trip to Chang Chang's home in Guangzhou; the chance that Kin Mou's old school mate might provide Suk Hing with crucial details to aid her escape outweighed the potential dangers, or the gnawing doubt that would plague her if she didn't take the chance at all.

While not a far distance, the bus journey from town to Guangzhou was expensive and tiring, punctuated by numerous stops and delays. Luckily, Suk Hing remembered where Chang Chang lived. As she made her way through the city, Suk Hing hoped that Chang Chang wouldn't be angry that her brother had spoken of her. Tentatively approaching the house, she knocked on the door and waited anxiously. When Chang Chang opened the door, she instantly recognized Suk Hing and greeted her warmly, inviting her in for tea.

After some enquiries into each other's health and the wellbeing of their respective families, Suk Hing got to the point of the visit. Chang Chang was very surprised and extremely wary until Suk Hing explained her brother had trusted her with the information that Chang Chang had contacts.

"Not so many girls attempt the journey, Suk Hing. Are you sure you want to do this? Are you strong enough?"

"I'm sure," Suk Hing replied with a determined lift of her chin.

"Fine, then tell me the date you will travel and the route you are taking."

Suk Hing went on to give her the details of the journey. The girl thought for a moment and then nodded.

"Yes, there is someone who knows a family on that route who are willing to help. I'll organize the place to stay for you. How many of you will there be and how long do you intend to be there?"

"There's only three of us, two guys and me, and we would like to stay two nights, if possible."

Chang Chang nodded again. She went on to inform Suk Hing of the payment each would need to make for the privilege of safe shelter. She explained that although many were against the government and were keen to help those brave enough to attempt escape despite the risks, times were desperate all round and money had to be made wherever it could. She told Suk Hing the thirty Yuan price included warm food and hot water for baths if required, as well as a comfortable bed to sleep in and gather their strength.

Suk Hing agreed upon the fee on behalf of the three of them, knowing her companions would be glad for a bed and hot meal by the time they reached the safe house. She was then shown on a map where the house was located, and told to repeat the information until she had it memorized.

"Don't write it down. Their lives would be in danger if this information fell into the wrong hands."

"I understand, and thank you."

Chang Chang waived her normal fee for setting up connections, but accepted it for the others, and they parted on pleasant terms.

"Give my regards to your brother if you ever see him again," Chang Chang called as Suk Hing departed for the long journey back home, repeating the new information in her head as she travelled. She had no real idea if she could trust Chang Chang, or the information given to her. The whole trip could have been a waste of money, or worse, a trap. She had to take the risk, though, and the excursion to Guangzhou had left her feeling a little more in control of the situation. There was less left to chance and her odds of survival seemed to have improved.

The time flew by, and soon it was the night before her journey would begin. Struggling to control the whorl of fear and excitement within her, Suk Hing made her way to the park, where she would take her final walk with Jin Jing.

"Jin Jing, I'm leaving tonight."

"Tonight! Suk Hing, that's wonderful! Are you sure? Will you be safe? You have your route, I guess. And your travelling companions, right? Don't answer, don't answer...I'm just..."

Jin Jing paused; there were tears welling in her eyes. She gripped Suk Hing by the shoulders.

"You'll make it. You're going to make it."

"Thank you, Jin Jing, for everything. Without you I couldn't have even come this far."

The two friends embraced.

"I hope I never see you again," said Jin Jing, half-joking.

That night, Suk Hing waited until her mother went to bed, and then crept into the large room that served as a kitchen. Her backpack sat in the corner, already containing two deflated ball bladders, her compass, and around thirty Yuan, which was all that was left of her savings after buying the necessary items little by little. She now had to prepare food. The others had given her advice on what to take with her. She mixed rice flour and sugar in a bowl with water into a stiff paste that she could squeeze into balls, quickly fry, and lay in rows to cool and dry out before she packed them. This was all she had to eat for the next week at least, but they were small and light, easy to carry, and the sugar and carbohydrates would provide her body with much needed energy, albeit in very small quantities.

Having done all she could for now, Suk Hing lay down to try and grab some precious sleep before it was time to leave.

Chapter Six

"If you don't enter the tiger's den, how will you get the tiger's cub?"

May 30^{th,} 1966, 8:30 PM

Suk Hing stood next to her sleeping mother. She knew she couldn't wake her to say goodbye. There was no doubt her mother would be questioned by soldiers once her absence was noticed. If they got the slightest hint that her mother knew something of her whereabouts they would punish her severely. It was safer for her mother to be able to say honestly that she knew nothing of what had happened to her daughter, or had any prior knowledge of her plans. As much as it hurt, she knew it was the best thing she could do for her now.

Tiptoeing across the wooden floor as silently as she could, she threw one last glance in her mother's direction, keeping her eyes averted from the poster of Mao as she left the room. Creeping out of the house, she closed the door for what she hoped was the last time. She swung her backpack onto her small shoulders, checking carefully for patrols before moving silently out into the early morning.

She held her breath as she heard approaching footsteps. Suddenly, this seemed all too real to her. Even through her desperation and desire, sometimes it had felt like a game, despite her head knowing otherwise. Now her heart truly knew of the danger she faced. The footsteps could belong to a soldier and if questioned and searched, she would have no explanation for the items in her backpack and her dream would be over before it had even begun. She darted to the nearest doorway and pressed herself hard into the recess, willing herself to become invisible in the shadows.

As the footsteps turned in the other direction and faded into the distance, Suk Hing breathed a huge sigh of relief. She pulled herself together quickly, telling herself she would never make it if she were going to fall to pieces at the slightest hint of a problem. She needed to be cautious, and stealthy, but her pounding heart and dry mouth were ridiculous, and her actions had looked very suspicious. She needed to do much better than that. Assuring herself she would be fine once she was out of her own little town, she set off determined to keep her wits about her from then on.

The first part of her journey was to be tackled on her own. She had no idea where her travel companions lived, but they were all taking different routes to an arranged meeting point. They had been advised by the group leaders that it was safer this way, as capture of one wouldn't mean failure for them all. Suk Hing had grown fond of the two young men over the planning period, and worried for their safety at this stage as much as her own, hoping that they could all make it to the meeting point without capture. She would have rather they all be in this together from the start, looking out for one another, but knew staying apart until they each reached the crowded city made sense and gave them all the best chance. She thought of them as she walked through the chill of morning.

They had decided that each of them would choose an easy name, one that could be called out, short and sharp. Her first companion was known to her only as "Hai." He was kind and pleasant, but a little frightened by the prospect ahead of him. He was probably the least physically fit of the three, and would always want to seek out the easiest options where possible. Suk Hing worried for him when she considered the physical nature of this voyage. He was also nervous and jumpy, and she would need to keep a close eye on him in public situations, ensuring he didn't give them away by his guilty and suspicious actions.

Her other companion went by the name of "Kang." He was incredibly outgoing and cheerful, possibly a touch too far on the devil-may-care side. If any of them were going to take risks, even unnecessary ones, it would be Kang. He was probably the strongest and fittest, and she would need to ensure that he didn't set a pace that was impossible for her and Hai to match and sustain. She had a very strong suspicion that she would need to be the voice of reason for one, and the voice of encouragement for the other, taking the middle ground and keeping them united.

Thinking of the new friends she would be meeting up with soon, Suk Hing couldn't help but turn her thoughts to the friends she was leaving behind. The sadness she felt at leaving them was mixed with fear of the unknown future, those two emotions whispering to her to turn back, to forget this and go home. At the same time, her excitement and determination drove her forward. The thought of a new and better life motivated her onwards, ensuring she kept a brisk pace.

It didn't take long for Suk Hing to reach the first milestone of her travels: the local ferry dock. She paid five Yuan and climbed into the small, wooden rowboat with a handful of other people. Once the boat held sufficient passengers to make the trip worthwhile, the ferryman jumped in and smoothly rowed the small, timber craft to the other side of the river. The twenty-minute journey passed in silence, people assuming others were making the trip to work in outlying farms and fields. Climbing onto the riverbank at the other side, Suk Hing congratulated herself on keeping herself calm throughout the crossing. She had made it out of the house and town without being spotted and raised no suspicion amongst the other passengers here. Reminding herself not to get overly confident, she maintained the attitude of a repressed worker as she made the fifteen-minute walk to the bus stop. It was a part she had played for three years, so it came naturally to her.

The wait at the bus stop was long and anxious. She was still too close to her residence and own people to be certain she wouldn't be recognized and stopped with too many unanswerable questions being asked. The bus was unreliable and its stops irregular, sometimes coming every hour, sometimes every two. There was no telling when it would turn up, or if there would be room for her to get on when it did.

When the bus finally arrived, just under two hours later, Suk Hing was relieved to find that there were indeed a few spaces left. Avoiding eye contact with the other passengers, Suk Hing inched her way to one of the small, empty seats. She was tired and wanted to sleep, but the journey to her destination was only one hour, and she was afraid she would sleep through her stop. Although she carried a compass, she didn't dare carry a map. If she deviated from the memorized path, she might never find her route again.

She exited the bus in the city of Guangzhou which was bustling and hectic, with a complex layout. Suk Hing didn't dare ask for directions as the dialect here was very different from the one she had picked up in the town over the last few years. Her speech would instantly mark her as an outsider, probably up to no good. It was likely that any local would be suspicious and report her to the nearest soldier. She walked for what felt like miles around the city, searching for signs that would lead her to the next phase of her travels, which was another ferry terminal. The ferry only ran once per day, and she was getting frantic that she might miss it if she took much longer to find its departure point. It was touch and go, but finally spotting the correct signpost, she increased her pace and arrived in time to catch the one ferry, which left at eleven p.m. She paid her fare and clambered aboard, settling down for the five-hour trip. The tension caught up with Suk Hing and she fell into a restless sleep.

Awaking an hour before the ferry was due to arrive at the large town of Rongqi Suk Hing was glad that this was the last part of the journey she would have to make on her own. This was where she was to meet her two friends and they would travel together from now on. Having company would make the journey pass more quickly and they would share the worry between them. Feeling her stomach gnaw with hunger, she popped one of her flour and sugar balls into her mouth, savouring it as much as possible before it dissolved.

At four a.m., Suk Hing disembarked the ferry and slowly made her way to the makeshift restaurant where she was to meet up with her companions. Her muscles had stiffened over the course of the passage and her legs ached when she moved, but she pushed through the discomfort, anxious to ensure that the others had made it. Arriving at the meeting place, she was relieved and pleased to see Hai already waiting, looking slightly nervous, but otherwise unscathed by his adventures so far.

"Hai," she greeted him warmly. "I am so glad to see you and so happy you made it."

"You too, Su," he replied, calling her by the only name he knew. "How has it been so far, any problems?"

"No, none at all, everything went according to plan. In fact, I seemed to get lucky a few times. I'm feeling very positive at the moment, especially after seeing you. How about you?"

"No problems, yet," he said, not quite as buoyed by his success so far as Suk Hing, knowing that the worst was still to come.

"Any sign or word from Kang yet?"

"No, not yet."

Just as Hai uttered the words, a lithe figure with a spring in his step bounded up to them.

"Well, well, fancy meeting you two here," Kang declared with a wide grin.

Reunited, the three felt more confident and at ease. They were now a long way from their respective homes, which offered them some security for the time being. They all knew the most dangerous parts of the trip were still to be faced, but for now, they could move forward with confidence.

"I didn't have any problems and don't think I was watched at all, anyone else?"

"No, we were both fine too," Suk Hing told Kang. "So next we make our way to Shiqi District?"

"That's right, it's probably a two or three day walk, but I think that there is an alternative."

"What's that, Kang?" Hai asked excitedly, eager to cut down the physicality of the trip in any way he could.

"See those guys hanging out over there with the scooters? They make money by being unofficial taxis. We could see if there are three willing to take us?"

"How much would that cost?" Suk Hing asked. None of them had a lot of money, and spending it so frivolously might not be an option. They wouldn't leave someone behind if they didn't have the funds to cover the fare for all three of them.

"Let me go and talk to them, I'll find out," Kang said, disappearing and making his way over to the group outside the makeshift restaurant.

They could see the frantic discussion, but couldn't make out what was being said. When Kang returned, he had his usual grin on his face.

"Good news and bad. Three are willing to take us as far as Xiaolan although it's an unusually long trip for them. It's as far as they are willing to go. They think it would be about a four-hour ride, so we could cut quite a lot of time off our journey if we didn't have to walk. The bad news is they want two Yuan per person."

Suk Hing grimaced. Considering she worked excruciating hours as a farmer for 75 Yuan a year, 2 Yuan for a four-hour trip was a lot of money to part with. Added to that, it was early days in the journey yet and they had no idea what they would face, so parting with that amount at this stage did not appeal.

"I think it's worth it," Hai said. "For the time and energy we will save. Can we all pay?"

They discussed their various options as the motor scooter crew watched them lazily, not pushing for the custom for such a long ride.

"Okay," Suk Hing finally agreed. "We'll do it."

After handing over the incredible sum of money, the three climbed on the back of the small mopeds and soon they were off. The vehicles were noisy, space was limited, and it wasn't the most fun or comfortable way to travel, but as the miles flew by, they all appreciated the speed they were moving. Suk Hing tipped her head back and enjoyed the wind in her face. It felt like freedom.

Climbing off the bikes in the small town of Xiaolan they checked their compass to get their bearings. They were all stiff and sore from the cramped journey, and their arms ached from holding on tightly to the bar behind them for so long. They stopped for a short while to rest and stretch their muscles. While they rested, they each ate one of their balls of food to boost their energy. They set off with renewed determination and high spirits. They were that much closer, and it spurred them on. Their next destination was in the area of Zhuxiuyuan which was another small town and the one where the safe house Suk Hing had hopefully arranged was located.

They chatted as they walked, their spirits lifted by the rapid progress they had made. After roughly three hours of walking, Suk Hing's shoes had worn through and her feet had become blistered and sore. She wished she had brought a spare pair with her, but knew that the extra weight would have added to the chafing of the backpack on her thin shoulders. She reminded herself they would soon be at the safe house, and they could rest for a while. At least, she hoped they could.

They continued on. Dusk fell and it became too dark to use the compass, so they let the few scattered lights of the next destination guide them. An hour later, they reached the small town they had been looking for. They spoke less and less and became more pensive as they drew closer. They still had no real idea if they could trust these people.

"Has anyone else considered this might be a trap?" Hai asked anxiously.

"Of course we have," Kang replied. "There is every chance that their real income comes from reporting people like us to the soldiers while we sleep in their beds."

"We could carry on and not stop, but we have been traveling for a long time. We're all hungry, filthy and sore. We could do with the rest here and a good night's sleep. We know what's ahead."

"I agree with Su," Kang said. "I would have thought that you, Hai, would be the one keenest to rest and be fed."

"I'm just afraid," Hai admitted. "We've come this far on our own. If we were captured because we were let down by others and through no fault of our own, it would be a double blow."

"It's a gamble, I admit. But I think we can trust them," Suk Hing said. "What do you think, Kang?"

"Nothing ventured, nothing gained," he grinned. "I say we check it out. If we are too suspicious, we can always run."

"Then are we all agreed?"

"Agreed," they answered Suk Hing in unison, and the trio carried on, following Suk Hing to the location she had memorized.

As they walked, Suk Hing thought back to the conversation with her brother. He had been certain Chang Chang's contacts would help, but he had failed in his attempt. She had no idea what route he had taken or at what point he had been captured. *Could it have been here?* she wondered. *Could he have been betrayed by these very people?*

She thought back to her visit with Chang Chang, how friendly she had been, and how concerned she was for the secrecy and well-being of her contacts. Suk Hing was hopeful they were making the right decision, and they had all agreed, but if they were captured here, she felt it would be her fault. She had arranged for all of this; her companions were relying on her. If they weren't safe, it was her responsibility, and the blame would fall on her shoulders if something went wrong. It would be a huge burden to carry for the next two nights, but she had to live with her actions, whatever the outcome. She grew more nervous as she followed the map in her head, leading them closer to the safe house.

They exchanged a glance as the address finally came into sight. Kang gave them an anxious grin and a shrug. His expression seemed to convey what they were all thinking: it was all or nothing now. They approached the door and knocked quietly. It was only seconds before the door flew open and they were ushered inside.

They had obviously been expected. The family welcomed the three refugees in, the lady of the house introducing them to her two sons and her daughter. Her husband was never mentioned, and Suk Hing wondered if he was away for work, or if the absence meant something more permanent.

"You must be so tired," the woman said kindly. "Oh, look at your feet, you poor thing. Come with me and we will run you a bath, you look filthy and your feet could do with a soak."

Suk Hing was led away, leaving the boys to fend for themselves and make conversation with the three children.

The bathroom was small but comfortable, and the rising steam of the bath looked like heaven to Suk Hing. Once the water was ready and the woman had taken away Suk Hing's soiled clothes and ruined shoes, she sank into the tub. Her blistered feet stung and burned, but the way the water soothed her other aches made whatever temporary pains she felt in her feet worthwhile. She lay back and let her mind drift, almost dozing. She welcomed the solitude at first, and then tears pricked her eyes as she thought back to her mother and friends back at home. This was the first opportunity since the early, solitary part of her journey she'd had to think of them, and she missed them all terribly.

Deciding she'd had enough of being alone with her thoughts, she was just about to step out when there was a gentle knock at the door. The daughter of the house popped her head into the room, peeping round the door.

"I've brought you some clean clothes; I think they will fit as we look about the same size."

"Oh no," Suk Hing protested. "I couldn't take those, it's too generous."

"Nonsense," the girl said. "I insist. Get dressed and come to the room straight across the hall, I have some shoes for you to try on and see if we can find a pair that fits."

The head ducked out again and the door closed, a neat pile of clothing left on the floor. Suk Hing dried herself with the soft, fluffy towel the lady had provided her and slipped into the clean outfit. The clothes were slightly too big on her tiny frame, but were comfortable and warm, just what she would need. Crossing the hall and knocking on the door, she was ushered into the girl's bedroom.

"These are the sturdiest pair I have. They are probably not much use for where you are going, but try them on anyway," the girl insisted.

Flushed with shyness, embarrassment and pleasure, Suk Hing tried the shoes on. Like the clothes, the shoes were slightly too big and slipped slightly off the heels of her feet as she walked. As grateful as she was for the girl's efforts, she knew that her heels would be rubbed raw and blistered in no time.

"That's no use, back in a minute!"

The girl dashed out of the room, coming back in with handfuls of thick men's socks. Giggling, the two girls layered the socks until the shoes fit, then chattered happily as they sat on the bed. For an hour or two, Suk Hing felt like the young girl that she was. A normal girl, living a normal life.

Chapter Seven

"Watch till clouds part to see moonlight"

June 2nd, 1966: 6:30 AM

Suk Hing woke up at dawn. Along with the rising sun and the birdsong loud in the nearby trees came a renewed sense of amazement and wonder, and a deep, unshakeable hope that everything would turn out fine. They had come so far; how could they not succeed?

Suk Hing felt rejuvenated, and on greeting the boys later, found they shared her enthusiasm. Not only had they had the first full night's sleep in what felt like a lifetime, but also they were safe, warm, and so much closer to their destination. The sunrise seemed to bring with it the idea of their fantastic dreams of a new life becoming a reality.

The two nights at the safe house passed far too quickly for them all. The family were kind and friendly, the food was good, hot and plentiful, and the house was comfortable. Suk Hing surmised that the family were far from wealthy, but they seemed to be doing okay. She didn't think that sheltering escapees could have been their main source of income. The refugees may have supplemented their income a little, but mostly the sum required covered their keep and only a little more. It seemed, rather, as if they risked themselves simply for the good they might do for others, rather than to make any kind of profit. Suk Hing was almost reluctant when the time came to leave. Before she did, she pulled the mother aside. Insistently, she pressed the money she had left of her savings into the woman's hands.

"This is too much, I can't take it," the woman cried.

"Please, it is the least I can do. It's only about twelve Yuan but it's all I have left. You have been more than generous, and it's the only way I have to repay you."

"Won't you need it?"

Suk Hing shook her head. "Our next stage of the journey is the most treacherous. We will be crossing the mountains to get to the coast. Money will be worthless in both locations. If I am caught, the soldiers will take it anyway, and I would rather have repaid you for your kindness than for them to have it."

The mother embraced Suk Hing. "Thank you, and good luck, I hope you make it."

As they parted, Suk Hing felt a wave of regret that she had never learned any of their names, but she supposed it was for the best. The two sons were waiting outside with their bicycles, and the three squeezed on. They were taken to the foothills of the mountain range they had to cross, and for fear of being spotted the boys didn't stop, merely slowing down enough for the three to jump off. As soon as they were clear, they watched the bikes speed up, disappearing rapidly into the distance.

The three looked up at the rough terrain. The mountains looked foreboding, but crossing them would lead them to the coastline, where they could leave mainland China for good.

Just as they began their climb, the weather broke. Huge torrents of rain fell, making it difficult to see more than a few feet ahead of them. They were only in the first hour of the most difficult part of the trip, and the dry warmth of the safe house had become a distant memory. The rain brought with it swarms of insects. Quivering clouds of giant mosquitoes plagued them at every step. It wasn't long before every inch of their exposed flesh became swollen with insect bites.

The weather tormented them for an entire week. They ploughed on, telling themselves the rain gave them extra cover that would aid them, despite the hazards and discomfort it added to their trek. None of them were equipped for mountain climbing and as the days and nights passed, they lost track of the number of mountains they scaled, blindly following one direction on their compass, rarely stopping to rest. They seldom spoke, each one concentrating instead on moving one foot in front of the other. Suk Hing's new shoes hadn't lasted long, and once again, her feet were blistered and bleeding. The extra socks had helped for only a short while, the material soon torn apart by the rugged, uneven terrain.

Just as they were beginning to think they would never reach the sea, they crested the next mountaintop, and the sea was suddenly in view. Collapsing with relief, they surveyed the final obstacles before them. First, there was the difficult, steep descent from the mountain. Then, there was crossing the roughly two kilometre area of flat land separating the base of the mountain from the seashore. A few small trees dotted the plain, but it was otherwise open and exposed. Worse, the distance was bisected by a well-trod one hundred meter trail, patrolled by small groups of soldiers. Finally, there was the ocean itself, dark and heaving in the stormy weather, as uninviting as it could possibly be.

Suk Hing, Hai, and Kang began their descent, glum and silent. Three quarters of the way down, they stopped again to better observe the military patrols. They could now make out that the soldiers beneath them were not only armed, but all had dogs by their sides, none of them restrained by a leash.

"We have to outrun the dogs. I think we can do it," Kang said.

Suk Hing wasn't so sure. The dogs were large, lean, mean and hungry-looking, with long, sturdy legs. One of them was sure to spot their movement or catch their scent as soon as they reached the foothills. Once there, they couldn't hesitate for a second, there was nowhere to hide.

"We should wait for the tide to turn," Hai said. "It's a twelve-hour tide, and in only one hour, it will change in our favour. That way, not only will we be better able to tell which direction we are going, it will pull us the right way on our floats if we get too tired to keep swimming."

Suk Hing and Kang looked at each other and nodded. They would wait out the hour and begin their attempt as soon as the tide changed. It would be a long, tense hour, but if it added to their chances, then it would be worth it.

The hour up, it was time to move. Just as they began to rise, a sharp peal of laugher cut through the stillness, echoing around the mountain. The three ducked back down quickly. Suk Hing plucked up the courage to rise and peek over the rocks. Dropping back down, she turned to Kang and Hai.

"Two soldiers standing talking, about two hundred meters to our left. Both have unleashed dogs by their side," she hissed urgently.

"Two hundred meters is a good head start," Kang replied.

"Yes, for a short distance maybe it would be enough, but for a distance of two kilometres, not a chance, the dogs will gain on us with every stride and soon catch up."

"I agree with Su," Hai was quick to add.

"Besides," Suk Hing continued. "The dogs will certainly follow us into the water. As soon as the waves are knee height, it will be as if we're wading through sand, it still won't be deep enough for us to start swimming safely. It will slow us right down, but the dogs will have no such trouble."

"But if we get to where we can swim, we can out swim a dog, surely?" Kang persisted.

"Dogs can be lazy swimmers, paddling only with their front legs, tucking their back legs up, but when they are chasing something, they kick hard with their powerful hind legs, which propel them forward at an amazing speed. We can't out swim them any more than we can outrun them."

Suk Hing and Kang sat in silence to digest this latest piece of unwelcome information. They couldn't outrun or out swim the dogs, yet they needed to do both in order to escape.

"We have no choice but to wait for these two to move on, and time it so that we have a larger gap between us and them," Suk Hing decided with a sigh.

Seeing no other options, the boys agreed. Almost two hours passed before the opportunity to run presented itself. The three looked at each other.

"Good luck, both of you," Suk Hing said, still doubtful that she would make the long sprint safely.

"Yes, and you, Su," the others said. They shook hands and held each other's eyes, conveying the unspoken final goodbye it would be if they didn't make it. Moving as stealthily as they could, they made their way down to the bottom of the mountain, stepping onto the flat land and running for all they were worth with no more hesitation.

As expected, one of the dogs caught their scent immediately. It began ferociously barking and dashed towards them, teeth bared and jaws dripping, alerting and attracting the other dogs in the area, and the soldiers. The three of them separated and fled in different directions. Suk Hing took quick stock of the speed of the advancing dog, and the distance she still had to cover. She knew she was never going to make it to the water. She changed direction, but the dog followed, zigzagging with far greater ease than she had. The dog rapidly closed the remaining distance. It leapt for Suk Hing, and sunk its jaws into her backpack. The pack fell from her shoulders, and Suk Hing continued running, never looking back. At that moment, she heard a sharp whistle somewhere behind her. The dog paused and turned towards the call, and Suk Hing used this small window of opportunity to frantically swerve and scramble back up the side of the mountain.

She found a place to hide a few meters away, in a bush that grew over and around a large stone. There was just enough room for Suk Hing to squeeze her tiny body into a gap between the stone and the hillside, crawling back as far as she could. She knew she would be out of sight of the soldiers, but if the dogs came back this way, they were sure to sniff her out, or hear her. If they did, everything was over. There was nowhere to run to this time. She was cornered.

Suk Hing hid for what felt like an eternity, listening to the shouting of the soldiers and the barking dogs, sounds which often seemed as though they were right next to her. Suk Hing held her breath, afraid to move for fear of giving herself away. She let out a gasping breath as soon as the sounds were far enough in the distance, trembling with fear and adrenaline. She had no idea what had happened to Hai and Kang. She hoped with all her heart that they had managed to escape, but she doubted it. There was nothing else to do but make the run again, this time on her own.

Some minutes passed before the noise died down. Night was falling, and the cold had set in. Before Suk Hing knew it, everything around her was pitch black. She knew she couldn't waste time searching for her dropped backpack. She regretted losing her float, surviving the swim might be all but impossible without them, but it had been the only course of action available to her at the time.

She crawled from her hiding place and threw herself down the mountainside, running at full speed, not daring to look in any direction except forward, towards the water's edge. The waves struck her knees with such force that they nearly ground her to a halt, her momentum carrying her upper body forward so that she fell face first into the icy sea. Scrambling to her feet, she moved as fast as she was able through the advancing and retreating waves, desperate to get deep enough to swim.

Finally, as the water reached her chest, it was deep enough. Flinging herself forward into the freezing blackness, she began to swim for her life.

Chapter Eight

"Fortune does not come twice.
Misfortune does not come alone"

June 6th, 1966: Midnight

Suk Hing swam for hours in the icy waters. In the distance, lights rimmed the heaving black. She felt a surging beneath and around her, the drift of the tide like invisible hawsers wracking her limbs. The delay had meant their careful planning around the twelve-hour tide was for nothing, and despite a hard-fought battle, Suk Hing hadn't been strong enough to overcome the raw power of nature. Eventually, her strength gave out. The tide would carry her wherever it may. The distant glimmer dissolved, along with her body, which felt suddenly weightless, and then all went dark.

She was roused back to consciousness by the sound of cocked rifles. Around her, a circle of soldiers in the half light, all pointing their weapons and shouting, as though Suk Hing was a dangerous criminal and not a young girl washed up from the sea. A rough hand pulled Suk Hing aggressively to her feet, and a gun pressed into the small of her back.

"MOVE!"

She walked this way for an hour and a half, trudging along as the soldier kept the gun pressed close to her. Suk Hing's limbs still ached from her failed swim and the punishing journey before it, but if she showed any sign of slowing, or if she limped or stumbled over her ragged feet, which still stung with the salt from the ocean drying painfully in her wounds, the guard would growl at her to keep moving, the only words he spoke on the trek. But Suk Hing's physical discomfort paled in comparison to the pain of her failure. She recollected where things had gone awry, how events had conspired to bring her to the threshold of freedom, but not beyond. She wondered what had happened to her companions. She wondered if they, or she, would be alive to ponder the fates of the others by morning, or if they all succumb to whatever darkness it was — sea, prison, or rifle slug — that awaited or had already overtaken them.

They eventually reached the outskirts of a nearby town, where Suk Hing guessed she would be imprisoned. Nobody in the town seemed to pay them any attention, the people hurrying about their business as the soldiers walked past with their prisoner. Suk Hing thought that the sight must be a common one.

It wasn't long before they reached a squat building surrounded by razorback barbed wire with armed guards on the other side of the vicious fence, the outside area teeming with what looked like hundreds of skinny, ragged people. She was led to a large warehouse style building, in which row upon row of cheap cot beds were crammed together.

Pushed roughly onto one of the dirty, thin mattresses, Suk Hing said nothing as the guard marched off. She stayed where she was placed, wondering what would happen to her next. She watched as eighteen more people were brought in the same way and treated just as roughly. Resigned, she gingerly tucked her feet up onto the bed and lay down, staring straight ahead, as others came and went, the prisoners obviously free to use the yard at their discretion.

At one point, someone arrived to clean and wrap crude bandages around her ruined feet, being none too gentle in the task and not uttering a word during their ministrations. Suk Hing glanced at him as he stood to leave.

"You need to work, so heal fast," he spat as he walked away.

Suk Hing sighed and closed her eyes, drifting in and out of sleep as the sounds of the prison echoed around her. She stayed that way for almost three days, only standing to limp to the filthy bathroom when necessary. She was mostly ignored by the other inmates and guards alike, and made no effort to change that situation. The longer she could stay under the radar, the better.

By the third day, the prison superiors deemed her fit to stand.

"You can stand, you can work," they told her.

Suk Hing was assigned two tasks. During the daylight hours, she had to cut hay by hand in the fields. She didn't mind this so much as at least she was out of the cramped and uncomfortable prison quarters and in the fresh air. The hay wasn't nearly as lethal as the sugar cane she had worked with before, and she already knew how to use a scythe. She would lose herself in the rhythmic movement of cutting, letting her mind wander as she worked, considering where she had gone wrong to end up here. After she had finished her shift, she had to help in the kitchen, performing any job that was assigned to her by whoever was in charge that day. She didn't like this nearly as much as being outside, where she could pretend she wasn't a convict and hadn't failed.

By this time, Suk Hing had struck up a few clandestine conversations with other prisoners, discovering that the large majority of them were escapees, and that over three hundred a day were caught near the place she had been discovered or nearby the surrounding coastline. She wasn't surprised to learn that so many people attempted the journey, but was surprised at the number who were unsuccessful. If it hadn't been for the tide, or if she could have fought against it for another two hours or so, she would have made it. She realized that she had gotten much further than most.

Whilst working in the kitchen one evening, she was surprised to encounter a familiar face.

"Hello, do you remember me?" she tentatively asked the boy working next to where she had been placed.

The boy glanced up, surprised at the female voice. "Yes! You stayed with my family. I'm sorry to see you didn't make it," he answered quietly.

"What are you doing in here?"

She looked at the boy from the safe house, taking in his gaunt form, calculating that he must have been living on meagre rations for some days before his appearance had changed so radically. The prison allowed them a lump of rice about the size of her tiny fist twice a day for their meals, and with most of the prisoners already being malnourished due to their lifestyle, and then the long journey from wherever they had started out, it wasn't nearly enough to begin the process of regaining strength.

"A day or so after we dropped you off at the foothills of the mountains on our bikes I decided to make the attempt myself. I thought perhaps I could catch up with you, but I was caught on the mountains before I even reached the shore. I was brought in a few days before you were."

"I'm sorry," Suk Hing said, remembering how well the family had treated her and thinking of how much distress the mother and sister would now be in, that is if they were aware that he was incarcerated here and now branded a traitor. The officials often neglected to inform anyone of the inmate's whereabouts. The family would be watched carefully now, so could no longer assist others by providing a safe refuge to prepare for the mountains.

A guard was heading in their direction so they dropped their heads and continued with their work. Talking amongst prisoners was a punishable offence.

They met up whenever they could, snatching conversations in low whispers. She learned that his name was Bui and, difficult as it was under the circumstances, they struck up a friendship.

"If I live, I'm trying again," Suk Hing informed him one day. They had to keep their sentences short, saying as much as they could with as few words as possible before guards were alerted and moved to separate them, usually with the barrels of their rifles or the back of their hands against their heads.

"Me too," Bui replied, his eyes burning with the same determination as Suk Hing's own.

The rest of their brief conversations revolved around plans for a second attempt, an agreement to meet up and go together the next time being hastily formed. Suk Hing was pleased with her new alliance and Bui became as close a friend as he could be under the restrictions of the prison. They always tried to sit together at meal times and he would often slip her extra food from his plate. He claimed that he couldn't stomach the bitter mashed turnips or other parts of the awful prison meals, and Suk Hing accepted his explanation as the truth.

The friendship and the plans kept Suk Hing strong, and she was disappointed when after one week and three days she was told to join a line of prisoners who were to be removed from the prison. She was ushered on to a military ferry along with hundreds of other prisoners and watched over at gunpoint.

During the awful journey, the prisoners were barely allowed to move, and certainly weren't allowed to talk amongst themselves. The prisoners sat, Suk Hing included, silent and unknowing of what their future would hold. They had no idea whether they were being transported to another prison, or being herded somewhere for execution. There was no one, and no way, to ask.

They travelled like this for two full days. When they finally arrived at their destination, Suk Hing struggled to get her muscles moving as the guards rushed them from the ferry onto the pier. Once disembarked, Suk Hing recognized the city as Guangzhou. She couldn't decide if this was a good or a bad thing. Was she being released, going back to live and work at home? Perhaps they were going to execute her in her own town square, making an example of her and using her as a deterrent for anyone else who might try to flee.

As she was marched along with the large crowd, Suk Hing's thoughts returned to her body, and all it had been through over the last few years. Her muscles had grown strong and taut while working in the fields, but the hard labour, combined with the meagreness of her rations, had weakened her already slight frame, and caused her to lose weight. Her body had stayed toned due to the work and the swimming, but the long treks, especially through the mountains, had ruined her feet. The following periods of captivity and confinement, coming immediately after such vigorous exercise, had caused her muscles to contract and tighten, and being forced to move suddenly with no chance to properly stretch them out was likely tearing something as she walked. She was absolutely determined to make a second attempt if her life was spared, but she wondered if she was going to be physically up to the challenge a second time.

The question as to Suk Hing's immediate future was answered as she and the others approached the foreboding walls of Guangzhou prison. Once inside, she was pushed into a dark, dirty cell; she was neither going to be freed nor executed, at least, not today.

The cell had no windows but was fronted with bars, allowing her no privacy whatsoever. It stank of urine. In one corner, lay a thin, stained and rank sleeping mat, in the other a bucket for her bodily needs. Suk Hing slid to the ground in the corner as far away as possible from them both, tucking her knees up to her chin and waiting to see what happened next.

Since the cell received no natural light, it was difficult to mark the passage of time, but Suk Hing had long since learned how to judge the speed at which it passed. She received two small meals per day – the portions smaller even than in the last prison – to help her keep track. Suk Hing remained there for an entire week, her meals shoved roughly through the bars without a word, the cell door never once opened. No exercise yard or opportunity to work outdoors were offered to her here, and she only had the occasional rat for company.

On the eighth day, she was sitting in her usual corner, in her usual position, when she heard a key in the cell door. Surprised, she looked up to see the door swing open. One guard entered the squalid cage while the other stood at the door, weapon at the ready. She was hauled roughly to her feet and dragged from her cell.

"Where are you taking me?" she asked, glad to be out of her cell, but wondering if this was the moment where she would lose her life.

If it was to be so, she had made her peace with it in the quiet contemplation that had been her only solace throughout the week, but she felt she had a right to know.

"Shut up and walk," the armed guard replied, stepping behind her and pushing her forward, the other leading the way.

Suk Hing was half-pushed outside, the bright light assaulting her eyes – which had become accustomed to the gloom of the cell over the week – and causing them to water. She blinked furiously, trying to clear her vision as she was led to a rickety old bus. The bus was already crammed full of people but she was forced to join them, the door slamming shut behind her.

"Where are they taking us now?" Suk Hing whispered to the nearest passenger.

He looked at her wide-eyed, and then shifted his glance to the guard that stood at the front, watching them all closely. He dropped his head and Suk Hing had no idea if he didn't know, or if he was refusing to answer. She had no choice but to wait and find out as the rickety bus began its bumpy journey, being met with guards at various towns and villages along the way, where one or more of the prisoners would be roughly escorted off, the bus driving away, abandoning them to their fate.

As they approached the outskirts of Haizhu District, Suk Hing thought that perhaps she was going home. Maybe she had served her sentence, been punished for her actions, and was now required to rejoin the working population, earning her keep as a farmer. With the number of prisoners she had seen captured per day during her initial incarceration it had to be a consideration that the country might be struggling, growing short on workers in various capacities. Not to mention the number who died every day due to starvation. If things carried on the way they were, the government might not have a population to rule over at all. The thought amused Suk Hing, and she gave a small smile as the bus pulled to a halt in front of the official government building in her town. As she was escorted from the vehicle and led inside, she knew she wasn't going to be let off so easily just yet.

The head government official of the town awaited her in a small, claustrophobic room. She was made to stand in front of his desk, a guard standing by at the door in case his services were required to make her talk.

"Tell me who helped you try to escape."

The demand came at her out of the blue, with no warning. They had hoped to surprise her into a giving up her contacts.

"No one, I went on my own."

Suk Hing had quickly decided it would be best to answer all of their questions, appearing as if she was fully compliant. She would use as many of the facts as possible, giving her answers the ring of truth, while ensuring that she didn't implicate anyone else. It wasn't because she was afraid to stand up to them by refusing to talk, but felt it was the best method of protecting the others. The more she refused to answer, the more they would assume she had something to hide. They wouldn't expect a young female to withstand their questioning; they would expect her to crumble immediately, so Suk Hing was merely giving them what they wanted, while keeping the information she most precious to her a closely guarded secret.

"Impossible! A female farmer, planning this on her own? Tell me the truth!"

"It is the truth. I travelled to the city where no one would know me and bought a map. I came home with the map and studied it, planning the route I would take. I saved a few Yuan wherever I could, preparing for the trip."

She knew her trip to the city could probably be discovered if they decided to investigate far enough. This way, she already had the cover story for her visit there in place, in hopes of keeping Chang Chang well out of the equation. If anyone knew of her visit to the woman's home, she would just say she looked up an old friend while she was there.

"You went all the way to the city to buy a map?"

"Yes, I'm known in many small places in the area, having worked on various farms with people from all over. If I had bought one in the surrounding villages, people would have suspected my intention and informed you. It was safer to go to the city, where I'm merely another face in the crowd."

"So you brought home this map and studied it, planning out a route on your own? How did you decide?"

"I took into account the methods of transport that were familiar to me to begin with, which took me to a city that was in the direction of the coast. From there, I plotted a route to get to the edge of the water."

"Tell us the route you used, show me on this map," the man said, pulling a crude map from his drawer and spreading it across his desk.

Suk Hing hesitated only a fraction of a second. The route she had planned with the group was designed to avoid many of the points that were already heavily guarded because they were known to the government. She and her companions had avoided the main ferry lines from Guangzhou that would have reduced their travel time by two full days for the very reason that it was commonly used and many were caught as they landed. They had chosen an elaborate and difficult way, one of the longest, in order to give them the best chance. If she revealed her exact route, it would be more closely watched in future; if she didn't, they might guess she was lying about everything. She wasn't afraid of possible torture, but she was afraid of breaking under it, and giving away those who had helped her. She decided to stick mainly to the truth, with a few small changes, and showed the man on the map as he had requested.

"Okay then, if you were so clever to work all that out on your own, talk me through it."

Suk Hing began with sneaking out of her house in the early morning, talking them through the walk to the ferry, the crossing, that walk to the bus and the wait at the stop, and then the bus ride to the city. She told it all with open honesty. At several points, they stopped her, making her repeat parts or confirm more details, hoping to catch her out in a lie, which they never did. She simply retold the same facts over again, never losing patience and never deviating from her story.

With growing confidence, she spun her tale of the long walks, the lonely and frightening trip across the mountains that shredded her feet; keeping all her companions and assistants to herself, even the motorcycle taxis. She was careful to hide her defiance and pride, allowing the man to believe she was afraid, spilling her guts because she was ordered to.

The man seemed pleased at the part of her story where she emerged onto the beach and was chased down by a dog and captured by the soldiers. She made it sound as if the beach where she had been apprehended had been her point of exit, her final destination before she attempted to reach the water. She didn't think that individual tales of capture would be remembered, as there were so many of them. Even if such stories were remembered, she doubted they would travel to the hometowns; the numbers were simply too high for that to happen.

Suk Hing could see no way that anyone could know just how far she had made it, how close she had been. Better to let them think she had only made it as far as the beach. She had been found soaking wet and exhausted, but that could just as easily have been from the rain and the climb over the mountains. The official was too pleased with the job of his soldiers to question that part very much. His arrogance was playing right into her hands.

The interrogation lasted over two hours. There were two main questions thrown at her constantly: "Who knew of your plans?" and "Who was with you or assisted you?" She continually stated that nobody knew of her intentions, that she had planned it all and travelled alone the entire time, speaking to no one on the way. When the official motioned to the guard, she thought the interrogation was over, but the official had other ideas.

Suk Hing was escorted to a large meeting hall and placed centre stage; while what felt like thousands of people filed in from all over town. In front of the population of the town, she was officially branded a traitor to the government, a betrayer not to be trusted by any of them. She was insulted and ridiculed. The official used every possible tactic to humiliate her in front of her former friends, family, and hundreds of strangers. Suk Hing refused to flinch as the crowd booed and jeered at her under the official's encouragement. Instead, she gazed directly into the eyes of people within the crowd itself. Mostly, it was the townspeople who looked away first.

The humiliation was followed by a rabble-rousing propaganda speech. The official concluded his speech by declaring Suk Hing *persona non grata* and issuing a stern warning of what might happen to anyone caught associating with the "traitor." The people cheered and applauded, as they were supposed to.

Suk Hing was led out of the square and into the same bus that had brought her there, her heart sinking with the realization that she was headed back to the prison in the city. Once there, she was escorted back to her familiar cell, and left to wonder whether any of the other prisoners they had dropped off and collected on the way had given them information that had made this entire farce worthwhile.

For three more days, Suk Hing had to suffer the stench and filth of her cell. She would later discover that this additional three-day waiting period was standard procedure. Once captured, prisoners often gave false names and addresses. In order to ensure the details they gave were correct, family members had three days to claim their relatives and prove their identity, after which the prisoner would be immediately released. It was a clever strategy, designed not only to ensure that the government had the accurate details on the defectors, but also the names and addresses of family members who cared enough to collect them. An entire family could then be more easily surveilled.

Suk Hing doubted anyone would have come for her, even if she had known about this procedure at the time. She passed the extra days in the cell in the same way she had passed the first stretch by tucking herself into a corner, and thinking of how she would make her next escape.

After the third day, Suk Hing was released. She spent the next several days in the city, managing to secure a few hours' work here and there to pay for board and lodging. The people she stayed with were good to her, and sympathetic to her situation. She almost considered not going home, but she was anxious about her mother and her friend, Jin Jing. When she had enough money saved, she said goodbye to the city and made the journey back to her hometown.

Chapter Nine

"To hit dog with meat bun"

July 7th, 1966

Suk Hing's homecoming turned out to be far from welcoming. As she walked through the streets to her mother's house, people she had known for years refused to acknowledge her. They lowered their heads, crossed the street, and generally did anything they could to avoid speaking or associating with her in any way. As she entered the house, she found that her mother also had little to say to her.

Suk Hing could practically feel the disappointment radiating from her mother as she entered the room.

"Hello," Suk Hing said quietly.

"So, you're back then?"

"Yes, if that's okay?"

"Might as well be."

That was the full extent of their conversation that first night. Her mother never said a word about her leaving, or asked a single question about what had happened to her in the time that she had been gone. Suk Hing was relieved: it wasn't a story she necessarily wanted to tell. She had done what she had to do, endured what she had to endure, but in the end, she had failed.

The next day, Suk Hing resumed her routine of heading to the town square to see if she was on the list of workers assigned jobs for the day. She found that the situation was the same as the night before, even with those she knew well. Nobody would speak to her. Through the crowd, one familiar face accidentally caught Suk Hing's eye, though only for a moment. And in that moment Suk Hing watched Jin Jing's face twist into a grimace of pain and sorrow and her eyes glassy with tears, before, like the rest of the townspeople, she lowered her gaze and turned away. Suk Hing didn't hold any ill feelings toward her; she couldn't. Her friend had risked enough to help her in the first place, and Jin Jing had contacts, and her own family, to protect. She couldn't possibly associate with Suk Hing anymore. It made Suk Hing sad, but it was to be expected.

The small crowd assembled around the chalkboard parted to allow Suk Hing to make her way through. No one wanted to come too close to her for fear of being accused of talking with her. As she scanned the board, she was disappointed to find her name wasn't on the list. As a defector, she knew that her food certificate would be revoked, stamped with the large red 'DENIED' across the page, but now it seemed she had lost the right to work as well. Given communism's commitment to the notion that one's very humanity is defined by productive labour, losing the right to work would be perceived as deeply shameful. Suk Hing couldn't have cared less about how she may have appeared in the eyes of the government, but she did care about how she would be seen by her friends, her mother, and the community. It wasn't only that she could no longer earn her keep, however meagre; losing the right to work meant that she was effectively cut off from any further contact with anyone who could possibly aid in her future plans to escape. Dispirited, outcast, Suk Hing made her way home.

She had only travelled a dozen steps before noticing the soldier following her at a short distance. As she reached her mother's door, Suk Hing saw him reverse course back toward the town square, and knew that her steps were very likely to be watched from now on. The contradiction burned within her: as an "undesirable" she was to be cut off, isolated from everyone, yet she would never be left alone. Her mother glanced up at her as she walked back in.

"No work?"

Suk Hing shook her head unhappily. "I'm sorry."

"It was to be expected, I suppose. I don't blame you, Suk Hing, but I wish that you had made it. Coming back here is not a good idea, and is bad for both of us."

"Where else can I go without a food certificate? Why it is so bad for you? What's happened since I've been gone?"

"Much the same as what happened to you out there this morning, I suspect. People have not been kind to me. They assumed that, as your mother, I had to know of your plans and was covering for you. I went through several interrogations by the guards and have been shunned by the people here."

"But I made sure you knew nothing!" Suk Hing gasped.

"I know, and I thank you for that much at least. However, most wouldn't believe it, and they were afraid to talk to me in case they or their families were implicated. Now that you have been caught and have returned here, eliminating all doubt concerning your disappearance. I can only imagine that the situation will get worse. There is nothing to be done about it except get on with life, which is what I have been doing, and what you will have to do, for the moment."

As Suk Hing listened to Nim Ping Kan's words, she felt ashamed that she had brought this treatment and isolation upon her mother. There was nothing she could do about it now, though, and she couldn't help but notice the phrase her mother had added at the end: *for the moment*. It was almost as though her mother was encouraging her to try again, to get out if she could and make a new life elsewhere. Suk Hing knew she would never tell her when she did, but the unspoken understanding was already in place between them.

Suk Hing spent the rest of the day in the house helping her mother, only venturing out once to go to the market with her. It was not a pleasant outing. The townspeople seemed to shy away from them, as if they carried some awful, highly contagious disease. People would cross the street to avoid passing close by and no one would walk too closely behind or in front, either slowing down or speeding up to keep a good distance away from the so-called traitors.

Although none of the townspeople would as much as look at them, they were closely watched. Every step they took was monitored by a guard, who made no effort to remain secret. Whichever one spotted them leaving their home followed them, ready to report anything even remotely suspicious or use any excuse to humiliate them in public.

Suk Hing and her mother didn't speak to each other during the outing, knowing that their every word was being overheard and noted. Even buying the goods was done in single utterances, the vendors handing over the items in silence. The only words spoken was the price they required. If they could get away with saying nothing at all, they did.

Turning away from the market with their small amount of supplies in their basket, their path was suddenly blocked by a soldier.

"Let me see that basket," he demanded.

Suk Hing held out the basket so he could clearly see the contents. There wasn't much in it, only small packages containing small amounts of goods, which was all they could afford. The contents could clearly be seen from where he stood, but he shouldered the rifle that had previously been pointing at them and grabbed the basket from her hand. He took each item out, examined it, and then tossed it on the ground before moving on to the next. Once every item was on the ground, he grunted and threw the basket down to join them.

"Pick it up," he grunted, taking a step back and training the rifle on Suk Hing again as she crouched to gather the scattered goods and place them back in the basket.

Suk Hing felt humiliated, but not afraid. As she crouched to gather the goods scattered across the ground, humiliation gave way to anger and frustration. *How dare they force her to live in a country she didn't want to,* she thought, *how dare they treat her like a criminal for simply trying to leave!*

She rose slowly, catching her mother's eyes as she did so. Although her mother was hiding it well, Suk Hing could see the glint of defiance in her eyes. At that moment, she was incredibly proud of her mother. She was an aging woman, not in the best of health, and had been shunned by the community from the moment Suk Hing had left, yet she had not succumbed. She did not tremble in fear and quake under the scrutiny of the soldiers, did not despair in her isolation from the townsfolk, and did not seem to blame Suk Hing for her plight.

In that fleeting glance, they spoke a thousand words to each other. They spoke of all their hatred for the government, how it had ruined their country and their people, of what it had done to their family and their lives. They spoke of how proud they were of each other, and encouraged each other to stay strong. Outwardly, they were powerless, but inwardly, they would never be broken by the hated regime.

Suk Hing and her mother walked slowly side by side, neither glancing at the soldier as they passed. He didn't prevent them, but he followed. As they reached their front door, they heard him call out.

"You!"

Suk Hing turned and looked coldly at him, saying nothing, wondering what fresh torment he had dreamt up for them.

"Report for work tomorrow morning."

She turned and walked into the house, giving no indication that she had even heard. Once inside, they stayed silent for several minutes, putting away their purchases, just in case the soldier had crept close to listen to her reaction to the outing.

Suk Hing crept along the tiled floor to the door and listened. She could hear nothing, no small sounds of movement that would give away a position, no breathing, just empty silence. Turning from the door, Suk Hing entered the front room and sat down beside her mother.

"I had thought that with so many fleeing, so many captured and so many dying, that farmers would be scarce. They need every able-bodied person they can out in the fields, considering that it is time for harvest. I am glad I will be able to work again. We need the money."

"It won't be like before," her mother warned.

"What do you mean?"

"Before, you had friends who you shared your day with, the time passed quicker and the work was made easier by companionship and perhaps even laughter, if such a thing can be found in these dark days. Now, you will be an outcast. No one will show you the ropes, or teach you time- and labor-saving techniques. No one will stand by your side and work with you as a team. You will be completely on your own, and the days will be long and the work even more back breaking due to the isolation."

"I can live with that, provided I can earn money."

"It won't only be that, Suk Hing. The jobs they will find for you will be the most unpleasant jobs they can possibly think of. What they really want to do is flog you in the streets, or publicly execute you, but they are still trying to convince people to love the government, so they can't go that far. They will find other ways to break you, though."

"Never!" Suk Hing declared. "They are nothing but cowards and bullies. They will not break me. They can break my body all they want, but they will not break my will."

Her mother said nothing, but gave a small nod, and the two worked silently to prepare the evening meal. It was a dish of the cheapest produce available, soybean and turnips. Once the vegetables had been prepared, Suk Hing would stir-fry them together, and attempt to make it palatable by adding spices. It didn't work; the dish was disgusting, but Suk Hing would not give the government the satisfaction of starving to death, so they both choked down the meal as best they could. Neither of them ever looked forward to it, no matter how hungry they were. Suk Hing knew that earning the paltry wage as a farmer again would not help their food situation. With her food certificate denied, the household could still only purchase rations for one, which was being split between two. Nothing could change that now; she had made her bed and had to lie in it. Her mother would be better off with her gone, and having her rations to herself. It only made Suk Hing more determined to try again.

Chapter Ten

"Behind every smile there's teeth"

August 2nd, 1966

Early next morning, Suk Hing and her mother were sitting in the kitchen, passing the few moments before Suk Hing had to leave to gather in the town centre to check the board and discover her tasks for the day. They were both surprised by a knock at the door. Suk Hing rose to answer it, stunned to see an elderly woman she knew well by sight from the street standing there.

"Hello. May I help you?" she asked politely, wondering if someone was ill and the woman needed her to run for help. Suk Hing had always thought the woman lived alone, but it was possible that there was someone housebound living in the house, someone she hadn't seen before.

"Hello, dear," the woman replied in a cloying voice. "May I come in?"

Suk Hing stood away from the door, and the woman entered.

"Good morning, Yanmei. What can we do for you?" her mother asked as the woman entered the kitchen where she sat. Her tone was civil but not exactly welcoming.

"I just stopped by for a chat, that's all," the woman was trying hard to make her smile natural, but there was a slyness to it that set both Suk Hing and her mother on edge. "I just wanted to see how you were doing, after that business at the market."

"Oh we're fine; I can understand why the soldiers need to keep an eye on my daughter, it's to be expected and is understandable. We were happy to cooperate, weren't we Suk Hing?"

"Of course, mother," Suk Hing replied meekly, following her mother's lead.

Yanmei's eyes narrowed and her face sharpened for a second, and then realizing her mistake, she put the deceptively friendly smile back on her face.

"Well, that's good, I'm glad it didn't upset you. What are your plans for the day?"

"Nothing, really," Nim Ping Kan said breezily. "I have some chores to do in the house, and then I will prepare the meal for Suk Hing coming home from the fields tonight. She is going back to work today."

Her mother's tone suggested she was pleased with the idea, that her daughter was now ready to knuckle down and resume her normal life, loyal to the state.

"Yes, I have to leave very soon; can I walk you to your door on the way?" Suk Hing replied, using her sweetest voice.

Yanmei had no choice but to thank Suk Hing and accept her polite and kind offer. The two left, and as Suk Hing turned to close the door behind her, once again she caught her mother's eye. The look they exchanged said it all. The woman had been sent by the government to check up on them, trying to befriend them and get them to reveal their true thoughts and feelings. It was obvious Yanmei had thought it would be easy, considering no one else would speak to them. She had thought they would be grateful for her sympathy and friendship, but she had been too obvious, too blatant. Neither of them had been fooled.

Suk Hing escorted Yanmei to her door as promised, thanking her for her visit and departing and wishing her a good day. As she left, she wondered how long it would take Yanmei to meet with a guard and report what she had learned, even if that wasn't much. She bet it wouldn't be more than an hour.

Suk Hing made her way to the town centre where the experience was almost an exact replica of the day before, only this time her name was on the board. She was assigned to a farm she had not been to before, and, thinking quickly, she scanned the names on the board to find one she recognized, picking the corresponding male face out of the crowd and following him. There would be no point asking anyone for directions, they wouldn't tell her, just leave her get into trouble and have her wages for the day lost if she couldn't find the farm or was late in getting there.

She kept her distance from the man but kept him in sight, silently walking on her own, a large circle of open space all around her. Ahead and behind, people walked in groups, talking and laughing as they strode along. As Suk Hing approached the farm she saw fields full of lychee trees. She had never harvested the fruit before and thought the task might be bearable, similar to the peaches she had picked with Jin Jing.

Taking her place in line, Suk Hing approached a farmer, who handed a large bucket and assigned her a field number. Once again, she had listened carefully and followed others, finding her way to the correct field where a guard pointed to a line of trees. Suk Hing swallowed hard. Up close, the trees were at least fifty feet tall. She could see others climbing them freehand, and then moving around in the high branches to fill their buckets with the pinky-red fruit. Taking a deep breath, Suk Hing climbed the first tree.

She soon got the hang of it, but it was tense work, being so high and often having to stretch beyond her natural point of balance to reach all the fruit. Unpicked fruit could be easily spotted from the ground and the guards would send her back up if so much as one were missed. The rind of the fruit was roughly textured and bumpy. At first, it wasn't nearly so difficult to hand as the sharp-edged sugar cane, but over time the tips of her fingers were stained red from handling so many of them for such a long time. Filled, the bucket became very heavy, and getting back down the tree without spilling the fruit was a fine art. Suk Hing worked hard, lost in thought, and as the movements became second nature to her she reminded herself that any new physical skill she learned might be beneficial to her in her escape.

Her shift over, she handed in her bucket and trudged back to the board in town. She was surprised by how much her legs ached, but concluded that she had been gripping the branches with her thighs more than she had realized. It was a little lonely, not having anyone to talk to as she walked. She missed Jin Jing. Her friend had not tried to contact her in any way since her return and Suk Hing had not tried to approach her either. Suk Hing knew she was always being watched, either by guards or by government sympathizers. She would not be responsible for anyone being reported as possible traitors simply because she missed them. She was on her own, and she would stay that way.

Suk Hing was disappointed to learn that she was back in the rice fields for the rest of the day, but at least it was work. She kept to herself and fell into the old routine of stooping, cutting the tough plants low, bundling them and knocking them against the basket to separate the rice from the crop. The labour was still arduous, but Suk Hing had endured it in the past, and she would again. Despite her previous experience, however, her first shift back in the fields was torturous, and straightening up after it was even worse. Her back throbbed and cracked as she stood up for the first time in several hours. She eased slowly into an upright position, gently rotating at the waist to loosen it. But the moment she straightened, she was shoved roughly from behind and ordered to get moving by a soldier gathering up the stragglers. Suk Hing stumbled forward, but managed to regain her balance. She thought she heard a snicker of laughter behind her, but she ignored it, holding her head high and walking as best she could back to the farmer to return her tools.

When she returned home that night, she was relieved to see a fire in the clay stove. She heated herself in front of it for a moment, allowing herself the brief luxury before she had to prepare the evening meal.

"What are you burning?" she asked her mother, surprised there was money for fuel.

"I went out today and gathered some leaves and sticks, laying them out in the sun to dry. I had others sitting by the fire drying too, but they're all gone now. I used the last of them just before you came home."

Suk Hing felt a wave of pity for her mother wash over her. Her mother wasn't well, but she was still trying so hard. Gathering sticks wasn't easy work, and her mother shouldn't have had to do it, not at her age and in her state of health.

"Were you followed?"

"Yes, but they kept their distance and didn't stop me."

"That's something I suppose," Suk Hing muttered.

Her mother didn't deserve to be treated this way. Suk Hing didn't blame herself; her actions were hers alone. She blamed the government for taking it out on the families of those who dared try and stand up for themselves. Before she had left, people had been talking about how much healthcare was improving in the country since the new government had come into power, how people were living better, and longer. Maybe they were, if they didn't starve to death first, but where was this great care for her mother? Suk Hing could see the deterioration of her mother's condition while she had been gone. Her mother's face had withdrawn, pale, and had become increasingly frail-looking, rawboned, skeletal. The stroke had left her with bad headaches, and they were becoming more and more frequent. She needed not only more food, but also a better diet: a healthy, varied one that provided proper nutrients and vitamins. She needed medicine for the pain, and a chance to live out the remainder of her old age in comfort and warmth, not scavenging for a few measly twigs. If only Suk Hing could get away and make a better life for herself, then she could provide for her mother. She would find a way to get money back to her, money to buy fuel to keep the fire burning, money for pain medication, and perhaps even find a way to set up a deal with a corrupt soldier to provide black-market food. She really felt that a new life for her would be a new life for her mother, too, and she could care for her better by not being there.

"So what was all that about with Yanmei this morning?"

"You know as well as I do what she was up to," Nim Ping Kan replied sharply. "She was trying to gather information."

"Yes, but why is she involved in this?"

"Her son is a government official. I have no doubt he approached her and enlisted her to spy on us."

Understanding dawned within Suk Hing. Of course, the government would not hesitate to use their friends and family as spies, coaxing them to keep an eye on people who were close by and send their reports back. No more needed to be said on the subject.

Life passed that way for Suk Hing for a while. She worked hard in the fields for the harvest and she came straight home after work, never going to the park with the others, never having a conversation with anyone. She was often followed, and any trip to the market usually meant a confrontation with a soldier and a basket inspection, with their goods tossed meanly on the ground. Other days, Yanmei would hover around, asking questions and pretending interest in what they had managed to purchase that day, inspecting their goods as closely as the soldiers did. Suk Hing and Nim Ping Kan followed all the rules, and were always polite to the soldiers and to the old woman, but they would often catch each other's eye and share a look of disgust behind their backs. Nim Ping Kan seemed to particularly despise Yanmei's involvement, a civilian who had no right to treat others as she did, sneaking around and spying on people, running back to the soldiers to report them. It sickened them both.

When the harvest was over, Suk Hing wondered which job she would be assigned to next. She was horrified to learn that she was to be put in charge of caring for a herd of cattle. It was the one job that everyone in the town hated, but she kept her face impassive and accepted her lot. She knew it was just another form of punishment for her to endure, and she would endure everything they threw at her. It was an isolated position, but that made no difference to Suk Hing.

The cattle needed to be milked and tended to every six hours. Suk Hing would trudge to the field at two a.m., eight a.m., two p.m. and eight p.m., carrying out the tasks and often lying down in the cold field to try to sleep once the duties were done. It was at least a half hour walk to the field from her home and sometimes, it didn't seem worth making the return journey only to leave again.

During the rare times she was at home, Suk Hing watched her mother's health further deteriorate. She was growing sicker almost by the day. When Suk Hing rose in the middle of the night she often heard her mother quietly crying. Sometimes she even heard her talking to father, like he was still present. Suk Hing couldn't always make out all the words, but she would occasionally catch snatches of the conversation. Sometimes, she would speak to him of the government, how they would all still be together if it hadn't changed. Sometimes, she would speak about how much she missed him. Other times, she would speak of Suk Hing, and how her mother wished she had had a better life and had been successful in her escape.

These conversations broke Suk Hing's heart. Her mother had seemed so strong and determined the day the soldiers had come looking for her father, searching the house. She hadn't had time to consider how much her mother would feel after her father's disappearance, or his subsequent loss. It wasn't a subject they had discussed at any point in their lives. The things Suk Hing heard made her all the more determined to try to help her mother and to never be afraid of the soldiers ever again.

As she walked to the fields the next morning, she pondered her mother's life. It had been a bad night. Her mother had been crying and "speaking" with Simd Sum Lee more than usual, telling him that she missed him and hoped to join him soon. Her sickness, and the fact that she was eating less and less, made Suk Hing wonder how much time she had left. Her mother had never spoken of her past, her childhood or her upbringing. All she knew of her mother's life was from after Suk Hing had entered it and was old enough to remember. She thought that perhaps it had not been a good history. Her mother obviously loved her, but found it hard to show that love with gentle words or physical affection. Suk Hing thought her mother may have been raised without those things in her life. The fact that she never retold a happy childhood memory or spoke of her life before her marriage probably meant that she didn't have happy memories to tell, and it was a time she would rather forget. It seemed the only happy times in her life had been short-lived, and she had known nothing but misery before and after. Suk Hing could follow that pattern, living the rest of her life in misery, her happiness being snatched away forever when she was just a child, or she could fight to break the misery, making a new life of opportunity for herself. But her failure had left her uncertain. Often, things seemed hopeless. And then, one day, she received a letter.

Chapter Eleven

*"Be not afraid of growing slowly; be afraid
only of standing still"*

August 29th, 1966: 5 pm

Suk Hing had been working with the cattle for two weeks when the letter arrived at home. She had no idea how or when the letter had come to her as it was addressed with only her name. It must have been hand delivered, probably at great risk to the sender. She held her breath and opened it.

"We're going on a vacation. If you're interested in joining us, we leave on September 1st. See you at Rongqi port at 4am."

Her heart leapt. It must be from Bui, the son of the family who ran the safe house she had stayed at during her last attempt. She had been beginning to wonder if he had forgotten her, or if it had been too dangerous for him to get word to her. Now here it was; she had not been abandoned by everyone after all.

She thought over the situation and like a surprise gun shot, her head jerked up and immediately realized the meeting date was only a few days away. She was excited, but also concerned. She only had a few Yuan to her name. It was not enough to purchase the items she would need for the trip and there was no way for her to get extra food to take with her. She couldn't leave her mother short of food in her current condition. She had no idea what she was going to do, but she had to go, no matter what. It could be her last chance, and the only way to help her mother.

The day seemed to fly by and Suk Hing had not thought of a way to gather any extra money. Approaching the soldiers for extra work in between her current shifts would be stupidity; it would arouse their suspicion and ensure she was even more closely watched than before. Asking anyone else in town for chores was also pointless; not only did no one have money to spare, they wouldn't risk consorting with a known traitor.

The next day Suk Hing panicked. She absolutely had to have the items she needed for the trip, meaning she had to have money. She considered her very limited options. She knew her mother had salvaged a few items from the original house, items that would have been very expensive to purchase at the time and might still be valuable now. Her mother had never spoken of these objects, but Suk Hing knew they were stored in a makeshift bunk in her bedroom. She didn't know if her mother was keeping them for sentimental reasons, as reminders of her previous life, or if she was hanging on to them as a way of procuring emergency funds if things ever became truly desperate. Perhaps it was merely a small act of defiance, hiding them from the soldiers who were seizing things of value. There wasn't much Suk Hing could do if it was the former, but she didn't think it was. She had never seen her mother take the items down to look at them, or heard her speak fondly of them. She had to assume they had been stored away as collateral to use if the occasion arose.

Suk Hing considered her impending "vacation" enough of an emergency to take one of these hidden objects now. Not only was she desperate, but her mother was acutely ill. If Suk Hing was to have enough time to get herself established elsewhere and send money back for medicine, she needed to make this deadline given to her by the unsigned hand.

Examining the contents of the bunk, Suk Hing found an ornate looking vase. It was about one foot high and six inches wide. It was of an unusual, deep burgundy colour and stood on a wooden base. She had no idea of how much it would be worth, but it was pretty and uncommon, some-thing she could hope to sell quite quickly. She remembered from the days when she was part of this community that there was one government official who collected antiques; and was passionate about his sideline. She had seen him since her return, so she knew he was still in the town. Praying she wouldn't be searched on this occasion, she hid the vase in her usual shopping basket and headed for town.

Luck was with her; although she was watched, she wasn't searched. If she had been, the soldier would have probably taken the vase for himself, or smashed it out of spite. She made her way to the town hall, thinking quickly about how she would achieve an audience with the man. Greeting the armed guard at the door, she asked to see the official by name.

"What is your business with him?"

"I have some information for him," Suk Hing replied meekly, keeping her head down and avoiding eye contact.

"What? The traitor turned informant, now that is rich!"

The man laughed heartily, not believing a word. Suk Hing said nothing, just silently hoping it would work out.

"What kind of information?" the man finally asked, breaking the silence, his curiosity getting the better of him.

"I'm sorry; I can't tell anyone but him."

The guard looked at Suk Hing suspiciously. "Wait here," he barked, disappearing inside the building commandeered as government headquarters.

Suk Hing waited nervously, anxious that another guard would question and search her at any moment, discovering the vase and her catching her out in her lies. There wasn't a single transgression, no matter how trivial, that she could make that wouldn't be treated harshly now. Eventually, the door reopened and she was ushered inside.

The government official dismissed the guard, demanding that he close the door behind him.

"What do you want with me, little traitor?" he asked harshly, towering over Suk Hing.

"I have something which may be of interest to you," she replied, quickly uncovering the vase.

The man's demeanour changed instantly, greed lighting up his eyes as he saw the item Suk Hing had brought. He lifted it carefully from the basket and examined it closely. His excitement grew with the detailed inspection.

"This is a very rare item. There were only a few of them ever made and the last I heard there were only four of them left in this country," he informed Suk Hing. She was impressed by his knowledge and excited at his words, surprised that he was willing to share the information with her. She nodded, trying to look like she knew the rarity and value of the item she had in her possession.

"I take it you are looking to sell it?"

Suk Hing nodded again, still keeping her emotions hidden.

"I should ask why you want to sell, and what you will use the money for. However, in this instance, I will assume you want it for black market food and say no more. I will make you an offer of one hundred dollars, and no more will be said on the matter. Do we have an agreement?"

Suk Hing couldn't help the shock that registered on her face this time. The sum of money was outstanding; it was more than a whole year's wages! The fact that the offer had been made so readily, and the fact that the official was willing to keep quiet about the transaction – and deal with a traitor to secure it – spoke volumes about the worth of the item she had taken. In less desperate times, she might have been able to secure five times as much. However, there was no denying that these were desperate times and the offer was a good one, far better than she had hoped. She accepted, and the trade was made.

She hid the money as deep into her clothing as possible and scurried from the building. There was always the chance that the official would betray their deal now that he had the vase in his possession. He could easily have her stopped and searched, declaring that she was preparing to run again. No one would doubt his word, especially if she was caught with that sum of money on her person. They would probably declare her a thief as well.

Heart pounding, she was stopped by a guard as she passed the market. He demanded to see the contents of the basket, and Suk Hing kicked herself for not having the forethought to stop and buy something as she had hurried by, intent only on getting the money safely home.

"You haven't bought anything," he said, seeing the basket empty except for the large leaves used to wrap things in. He looked at her suspiciously.

"I wanted to buy some fish for my mother, but I found I didn't have enough money," Suk Hing replied, frantically thinking of a way to explain the empty basket. She'd had so much practice of hiding her true feeling in her nineteen years that she was becoming an accomplished liar. She felt no guilt lying to these cruel men. Fate seemed to smile on Suk Hing once more. The guard accepted her explanation and waved her on her way. She scurried home, desperate to relieve herself of the incriminating bundle of dollars.

Her mother wasn't at home when she got there. Suk Hing assumed she must be out gathering twigs for the clay burner, which was not yet lit for the day. Kneeling on the ground, she lifted a loose clay tile under the stove and laid the money flat, replacing the tile and ensuring it lay flush before breathing a huge sigh of relief. For now, she needed to get to the field and carry out her duties, maintaining her cover of the good little milkmaid adhering to all the rules.

The next day, when she rose for her two a.m. shift with the cattle, she removed forty dollars from the stash under the tile, leaving the rest in place. She saw to the animals as usual, then lay down to sleep in the field, awaking to perform her next set of duties a little earlier than normal. When they were done, she headed into the main part of town to purchase a sturdy pair of shoes, a football bladder, and a backpack. She bought each from a different place, hoping she could avoid raising too much suspicion, or being remembered by the vendors. She would need her mother with her later to buy food using her certificate, and for now, she could hide these items, provided she could make it home with them. She made it safely back, and later, when her mother accompanied her to the market, she made no comment on the flour and sugar that Suk Hing bought in addition to their usual supplies, nor did she ask where the funds came from to be able to afford them.

She carried out the rest of her shifts with the cattle as normal that day, trying to pretend that everything was fine, hiding her excitement inside from anyone who may be watching, treating Yanmei and even her mother the same as she generally did. This time, she felt absolutely no fear, only cold, hard determination.

Chapter Twelve

*"We have two lives, and the second begins
when we realize we only have one."*

August 31ᵗʰ, 1966: 7 AM

After carrying out the shift with the cattle in the early
hours of the morning, Suk Hing returned home and prepared her flour balls as she had done before, and checked
the contents of her new backpack. Everything was set.

She waited until it was around seven a.m., a time she
could reasonably pass off as time to head to the field to
see to the cows again. Her mother was awake and in the
kitchen. There could be no doubt that she had spotted the
backpack sitting on the floor there, but she didn't mention
it and neither did Suk Hing. Sitting at the table with her,
she confessed to the taking of the vase from her mother's

belongings, telling her she managed to sell it. Nim Ping Kan said very little about the matter, and Suk Hing hoped it was because she didn't care about the item that much.

"Underneath a loose tile under the clay burner there is $60. You should use it to buy some good food and maybe some medicine," she pleaded.

Her mother simply nodded, barely touching her breakfast.

"Don't use too much at once, though, we don't want anyone questioning where we got the money, so we can't attract attention to it. The government official I sold it to made me a deal, and part of that deal is that we keep quiet and never mention it to anyone."

Still, Nim Ping Kan made no comment but when Suk Hing announced she should leave for work, they held each other's gaze. In that moment, she knew her mother had full knowledge of what was happening this morning, and the less of a final conversation they had the better. She broke eye contact and slipped the backpack on, heading out the door once again.

She began to make her way to the ferry point, the same one she had used the first time she had left. It really was the only way to get to the bus she needed to board to take her to the city. As she crossed the bridge to reach it, she was stopped by someone she knew from the town. The man was a well-known government sympathizer, and Suk Hing knew she could be in trouble already. She tried to put a pleasant, open expression on her face as he spoke.

"Where are you heading anyway at this time of the morning?" he asked, finally dropping the small talk and asking what he really wanted to know.

"Oh, I received a letter from the police at Guangdong," she replied sincerely. "When I left prison, I wasn't allowed to take my belongings, but now that I am home and working again, they have instructed me to collect them. That's where I'm heading today. If I don't pick them up, they will be destroyed."

The man looked at her suspiciously, trying to determine if she was telling the truth.

"Do you have the letter with you?"

"Oh no, I didn't keep it, I'm sorry. I thought it was such a standard procedure that everyone would know."

Suk Hing knew that the man considered himself well liked and respected by the authorities and believed himself to be important. He wouldn't dare admit that there might be a procedure he had no knowledge of; if it turned out to be true, he would look foolish. Unfortunately, the man was shrewd and in turn, used her own tactic against her.

"I take it you have filled out and put up all your repentance posters that are required?"

Suk Hing was stuck. She had never been asked by the officials or the soldiers in town to do this, and had no idea if this was a genuine requirement. If he had made it up, then she would be caught in a lie if she told him she had already completed the task. She had no choice but to admit the truth.

"I'm sorry, I don't know what you're referring to," she told him meekly. Challenging him would only attract attention and raise suspicion so she had to play along.

"You must make your official apology to the town," he informed her grandly. "You must write out twelve posters, one for each district, and display them on the chalkboard of each area. I'm surprised you haven't already done this; you should have been made to do it as soon as you arrived home. It's a very important task which you must complete as soon as possible."

"I was not aware of this; I will go back right now and take care of it."

Suk Hing had no choice. She turned and ran back towards town, stashing her backpack in the bushes once she was out of sight of the interfering civilian, and before reaching the main streets of her home. She didn't have very much time, she needed to take the local ferry, then catch the same unreliable bus into the city in time to catch the main ferry which only ran once a day. If she missed it, she would miss her meeting time with Bui. She knew he wouldn't wait; he would have to assume she had been captured, and would leave without her. Reaching the government building, she gasped out her request for repentance posters to the guard at the door, wondering if he would laugh at her and say he had no clue what she was talking about.

To her surprise, he nodded and disappeared into the building, returning with a bulky roll of paper and a pen. After giving her the instructions, Suk Hing found a quiet spot and unrolled the bundle, staring with despair at the three-foot-by-three-foot posters. She knew there were twelve of them, and knew what she had to write on each. But she wasn't good with letters; writing was not her strongest subject in school. If she took the time to do all these, there was no hope of her catching the ferry in Guangdong.

In a desperate panic, she did the only thing she could think of. She ran to Jin Jing's house and knocked on the door. She was very lucky that the harvest was over as Jin Jing was at home. Her face displayed shock and surprise when she opened the door and saw Suk Hing standing there.

"What are you doing here? Come on, get inside, quick!"

She ushered Suk Hing inside and closed the door quickly behind her. Suk Hing was glad to find themselves alone in the house. In the privacy of the home, they hugged warmly.

"I've missed you so much, Suk Hing," Jin Jing said as she held on to her tightly.

"I've missed you too. You have no idea how many times I've thought about you or longed to have you by my side."

The girls had tears in their eyes as they pulled apart, and they each wiped their faces, slightly uncomfortable with their show of emotion.

"I'm sorry you didn't make it, Suk Hing. I was very optimistic for you. In many ways, it was horrible to see you back here, but I was so glad to see you were safe, too."

Suk Hing nodded but didn't comment. The less she spoke of that time, the better for her friend. If she had only come here for help with her letters, then she couldn't reasonably be punished. However, she thought it only fair to tell her the truth so she knew what she was getting involved in this time.

"I'm really sorry I had to come and involve you in my drama, but I didn't know what else to do," she said frantically, wringing her hands.

"What's wrong?" Jin Jing asked, the concern for her friend evident on her face. "Come on, Suk Hing, tell me. You obviously need my help with something or you wouldn't have come here. I know you too well, so out with it!"

"I'm sorry, I shouldn't be telling you, nobody knows, but I'm supposed to be leaving again today. I'm meant to catch the ferry then get to the city, taking the main ferry from there and meeting up with a companion. I was almost there, on the bridge, when Tin Guang stopped me."

Suk Hing's friend openly displayed her disgust when she mentioned the name.

"That man is a creep," Jin Jing said. "He ought to be ashamed of himself, sneaking around and betraying his own people the way he does. We should stand united, even if it is in secret, yet we have dogs like him who crawl on their bellies, trying to befriend the monsters who enslave us, spying on us and reporting our every word and every move."

Suk Hing nodded her agreement at her friend's outburst.

"So what happened when he stopped you?"

"He asked me a lot of questions, and when he wanted to know where I was going I told him I had to go into the city as I'd had a letter from the police saying I had to collect my belongings from prison before they were destroyed. I am glad he didn't ask what those belongings were as I only had the clothes I stood in!"

"It wasn't too bad a cover story, but it didn't work?"

"Well, yes and no. He wasn't sure whether to believe me or not and asked to see the letter. I said I didn't have it as it was such standard procedure I didn't think I would need it to prove my actions."

"Ha! I bet that foxed him," Jin Jing said. "That was quick thinking, Suk Hing; it put him in a corner."

"It did, but then he outfoxed me too, asking if I'd done my repentance posters. I had never heard a word about them, and didn't know if he was making it up or not. I had to say I would come back and do them immediately; there was no other option. It turns out it is true, the government would have asked me to do them eventually I suppose. Now I have to fill out twelve of these massive things and put them up on the chalkboards in each area of town!"

"So you want my help to write them out?"

Jin Jing grinned at her friend, knowing that she was not that good at writing. Schooling for those born after the new regime had taken control wasn't considered that important. As they would all end up as laborers anyway, there wasn't much point. The teachers had concentrated on propaganda, ensuring they delivered a batch of willing workers to the soldiers. Suk Hing was young enough to be part of that ethos.

"Yes, please!" Suk Hing said. "If I do them myself, I will never make the ferry, and if I don't make it, I'll miss the meeting time and I'll be left behind."

"Well, come on then, let's get them done."

Jin Jing hunted for another pen and they each took a poster, unrolling it flat on the floor while they knelt over it.

"So what do we need to write?" she asked.

"I have to fill the entire poster with the words so we need to write big letters for speed. I have to write three things until the page is full. 'I am sorry for what I have done. We have a good government and they teach us good things. Do not do what I did.'"

Jin Jing snorted. "So we have to fill these posters with lies as usual. Our whole lives seem to be made up of lies and distrust, however, this is no time for a political discussion, let's get writing."

Even with their combined efforts, it took over two hours to complete them. Suk Hing had no idea how long they would have taken her to do on her own, but she knew she wouldn't have been able to finish them in one day. She couldn't thank her friend enough for her help.

"Don't be silly," Jin Jing said. "It was the least I could do. What happens now?"

"Now I have to put them up on the twelve chalkboards in the twelve districts of town."

"You're never going to make it, Suk Hing. Here, give me half. You do the areas closest to where you live so you are seen by lots of people doing them, and the areas closest to the ferry. I'll put up the rest for you," she said, taking charge.

"I can't ask you to do that!"

"No arguments, there's no time, just make sure you catch that ferry," she grinned back at her. "If anyone comes to ask about your visit, I'll just say you couldn't remember your letters and you needed me to write it out once so you could copy it. I'll make it sound like I really approve of these posters, that I'm glad you've seen the error of your ways and that I was pleased to help in your repentance.

I'll say the same thing if I'm questioned when putting up the posters. If we stick to our story, it might keep us out of trouble, for a while anyway."

Jin Jing grinned cheekily then flung herself at Suk Hing, hugging her tightly. "Just make it this time. I don't know what will happen to you if you are caught again," she sobbed through her tears.

"I will," Suk Hing said, knowing she could promise no such thing, but anxious to comfort her sobbing friend.

They left the house together, each hurrying to their first destinations. Suk Hing tried to look ashamed and repentant as she scurried from one point to the other, hoping that all who saw her put her speed down to embarrassment of the task she had to do. The town felt twice the size as it normally did as she hurried around the six different districts with their work schedule chalkboards. She couldn't thank Jin Jing enough for her assistance in putting up the others. She was one of so many who were willing to put themselves at risk to help others. Suk Hing knew that all these people would live in her heart forever.

After tacking up the last poster, Suk Hing stood back and smiled, as if admiring her work. She was actually wondering about the best route to take to make it out of the town without being seen all over again. She turned and walked purposefully, hoping to keep the anxiousness she felt inside from showing. The further out of the main town she managed to get, the easier it became. Taking a few cautious glances over her shoulder when she reached the place where she had stashed her backpack, Suk Hing saw that she was alone. She quickly snatched it from the bushes and made her way back to the bridge, hoping that the horrid man was long gone. There was no sign of him when she crossed the bridge, or at the ferry, and she made it on board without any further problems.

Even when she disembarked the ferry at the other side, there was no chance to relax. She hurried to the bus stop, conscious of the tight deadline to make to the once-a-day ferry. The wait for the bus seemed to last forever. Her heart beat harder every time another person approached the stop. There were no familiar faces though, and she climbed on the bus gratefully when it eventually turned up.

The journey passed in the same way as it had the last time, with Suk Hing tired but too fearful of missing her stop to sleep. The morning had been an emotional one, with painful goodbyes and the stress of being caught almost straight away. Somehow, thanks to her friend, she had made it this far.

Chapter Thirteen

"A single slip may cause lasting sorrow"

August 31^{th,} 1966: 6 PM

Upon reaching Guangzhou, she discovered she actually had more than an hour before the ferry was due to leave. She felt it would be unwise to loiter around the dock area, knowing it would be well guarded by soldiers. The longer she stood around on her own, the more chance there was that one of them would question her. As accomplished an equivocator as Suk Hing had become, there really wasn't a plausible explanation for the items in her pack; it was one of the dangers of travelling with them. If she was searched, it was all over. Suk Hing had no real idea of what would happen to her if she was caught a second time.

She needed to go somewhere in the city to pass the time before arriving back at the ferry in time to blend in with the crowds who would be boarding. It wasn't safe to simply wander the streets. She knew she had a sister-in-law that lived nearby, but the possibility of stopping in only crossed her mind for a fraction of a second. Visiting would not only make her sister-in-law an accomplice, it would also place a definite sighting and timeline on her movements. With this second escape attempt, the stakes were different. The mere fact that Suk Hing would make a second attempt would be considered a major failure, one that the government would not take lightly. To let it be known that their years of propaganda had failed and that their imprisonment, humiliation and ostracization techniques had done nothing to change her feelings would be unacceptable to them. There was no doubt that once the alarm was raised that Suk Hing was missing yet again she would be actively hunted. They would want her back in their clutches to make an example of her, by whichever method they saw fit.

No, she couldn't go to her sister-in-law. The only other place Suk Hing could think of was her old family home. She had no real idea what had happened to it after Kin Mou had left, but the rooms they had been allowed to keep may have still been empty. And this time Suk Hing knew exactly where the terminal was and how long it would take to get back there from the family home. Concluding it was her best option she made her way there, hoping to hide out and maybe eat while she passed the time.

She approached the building with caution. How many of the rooms were occupied? She recalled there was one man living in the building who seemed to be a civilian but worked for the government. She used to encounter him often when making the weekend trips from her grandmother's farm to stay overnight and make appointments with the doctor for her mother. Suk Hing had never liked him, and had tried to talk to him as little as possible. She wasn't sure, but she thought he might have been a soldier at one time, perhaps wounded and retired early from the army. She was certain he had been housed there to report on the other residents. She didn't know if he would still be around but she knew she wanted to avoid him at all costs if he was. Darkness had fallen by the time she had arrived and the complex was eerily silent. She managed to make her way into the building and up to the room without encountering another living soul, but she couldn't be certain that she hadn't been seen.

Entering the room, Suk Hing was overcome with sadness. The room was musty, with thick layers of dust covering every inch. For a room that had once been a part of a vibrant, thriving, family home, it was now an empty shell, any happiness it once contained long gone. It seemed to sum up everything about her life from the day her father had disappeared.

Suk Hing sat on the dusty floor. After about twenty minutes, she treated herself to one of her balls of fried dough. As it dissolved slowly in her mouth, she heard footsteps and raised voices outside. She quickly swallowed what was left of the fried dough in her mouth, grabbed her backpack, and leapt to her feet. She didn't know what was happening, but she felt she would be safer outside, where she could run if necessary.

Opening the door of the room a crack, she peeked into the hallway. The corridor was still and silent. Suk Hing slipped through the door and crept her way along the hall, praying that no other heads would peer out of doors to investigate the source of the commotion. She tried to keep her breathing slow and steady as she eased down the stairs and moved towards the front exit, her back pressed firmly against the wall.

The voices were louder now. Suk Hing felt certain it was soldiers who were doing all the shouting; she recognized the scornful and derisive tones. Hesitantly opening the front door, silently willing it not to creak, she looked outside. To her right, by the entrance of the compound, she saw a group of soldiers standing in front of the man she remembered as an informant. The man looked nervous, and she could tell the soldiers were not being friendly. She continued edging the door open until she was able to slip through the tiny gap she had created and move away from them. Every instinct told her to let the door go and make a run for it, but she knew the sound of it closing and any sudden movement was more likely to attract attention. She softly guided the door back until it closed with a soft click and, with her back against the outside wall, inched her way along to the left of the man and the soldiers. As Suk Hing moved quiet through the dimly lit street she made sure to avert her face, knowing she could be easily recognized anywhere near her old home, but it was difficult not to look in the direction of the soldiers. With every step she expected to hear a sharp yell ordering her to stop. When she made it round to the side of the building without hearing the fateful call, she picked up speed, weaving her way through the sprawling complex, making her way back to where the soldiers stood, blocking her potential escape. From her vantage point on the opposite side of the street from her house, she could now clearly hear what was going on.

The soldiers were asking questions about people who lived in the complex and specifically asking for her family by name.

"Yes, they have a room here, but no one has lived there for a long time. A boy stayed here for a while, and the sister and mother used to travel to visit him, but once he left, no one ever came back."

"Where does the family live now?" the soldiers asked him.

"I don't know, they never left a forwarding address," the man answered, concerned that he couldn't give them the information they wanted. It was obvious he didn't like not knowing something or letting them down.

"Which room did they live in?"

When the caretaker gave them the directions, the man in charge ordered two men to check it out, the others remaining with the caretaker, questioning him about any movements in the complex that night.

"I haven't seen anyone tonight," he informed them, but when the two soldiers returned, they declared that there were footprints and disturbed dust all over the room, that someone had been there very recently.

The caretaker denied all knowledge, adamant that he had seen and heard nothing on his rounds. Suk Hing heard him beg and plead as the questioning intensified, and the man continued to swear he had no idea that the room had been used, or who might be responsible for it. The next order sickened her, as soldiers went to the caretaker's home and dragged the man's wife out into the street to join them. She too begged and pleaded that she was innocent of any wrong-doing, that she knew nothing of what they were asking. Suk Hing covered her ears to muffle the gruesome sounds of a severe beating and the screams of the husband and wife as the soldiers punished them relentlessly. While Suk Hing's mind told her that the beating went on for something like ten minutes, it felt like forever.

The soldiers were finally satisfied that the couple were telling the truth, their pleasure sated with violence. Determining they had nothing more to gain, they departed, presumably to report their findings, and the couple, dazed and bleeding, staggered woozily off the ground and into their home. Suk Hing knew there was nothing she could do for them. Any assistance she could offer would only make their situation worse. She also knew that the delay had cost her precious time and that she now ran the risk of missing the ferry once again.

Once all had been quiet for a few minutes, Suk Hing made a sprint for the exit from the compound. High profile and suspicious, there was nothing else for it but to keep running. She didn't take the time to look for soldiers, or to check and see if she was being pursued, she just ran, keeping her mind focused on her destination, weaving her way through the city streets. She made it just in the nick of time to the one and only boat leaving that day, just as it about to depart Guangzhou.

She practically threw herself onboard, and gasping for breath, made her way to a secluded corner to recover. She had no idea how she had escaped detection back at the house, or how she hadn't been spotted as she ran, but unless she had been followed and authorities had been alerted at the other end, she had, somehow, made it out of the city.

Suk Hing tried to sleep to pass the long hours of the crossing, but every time she closed her eyes she heard again the sounds of the terrible beating and experienced the grotesque images her mind conjured up to accompany them. Though Suk Hing knew she wasn't to blame for the soldiers' cruelty, she couldn't help feeling a pang of guilt and sorrow for the plight of the caretaker and his wife. She had no idea that using the old room would bring about such consequences, and it served as a harsh reminder of what exactly she was fleeing from and what would happen if she were caught. With sleep evading her, she tried to concentrate on her surroundings, but her own dark thoughts kept forcing themselves before her. The worst-case scenario, short of actually being caught, had come to pass. Someone had noticed her absence from the town and her alibi had been exposed. She was now actively being hunted by the government and orders had already spread as far as her old residence. They were close on her tail; things would be even harder from here on in.

The rest of the journey was uneventful, but Suk Hing grew nervous as the ferry approached Rongqi port. Would it be lined with soldiers, waiting for her to disembark so they could snatch her, or would she only see her old friend, as arranged? She hoped that if Bui was there, he would have the presence of mind to notice whether there were more soldiers about than normal, and that he would have the sense not to endanger them both by attempting to meet her. As the boat pulled into the dock, Suk Hing pressed deeply into the crowd of passengers gathering at the side of the ferry to wait their turn to step onshore, occasionally stealing a glance toward the wharf to see whether she could determine any potential threats waiting for her on shore.

It didn't look as if the docks were geared up for a manhunt. There were no more soldiers than usual, no fierce dogs straining at their leashes, anxious to be set free to chase down their prey. Instead, she was relieved and overjoyed to see Bui waiting patiently on the harborside with his pedal bike, just as he said he would be. She was careful to walk casually as she approached him, trying not to attract attention as she maneuvered herself onto the bike. Bui peddled out of the area as quickly as possible. They didn't talk much on the journey; Suk Hing concentrated on holding on to Bui while the two moved swiftly through the streets until they were clear of the city. Suk Hing offered to take a turn, but Bui refused, insisting on pedalling the entire five hours it took to reach his hometown near Zhongshan.

As they reached the outskirts of town, Bui slowed his pace and they cycled idly around.

"We have to wait for darkness," he explained. "We can't be seen going into my house together. I've been through my various punishment and atonement programs and am now supposedly integrated back into society, but the family is still under close watch. Thank you for not giving us up. I couldn't have stood watching my mother and sister punished for harbouring fugitives. I know firsthand what they must have put you through, so it would have been hard to keep quiet."

"Of course I kept quiet! I would never have betrayed anyone who helped me. I'm just sorry we both got caught."

They continued to talk in hush tones to pass the time as they cycled, keeping silent when they were in residential areas where they might be overheard.

As they cycled, Bui's attention was taken by something lying at the side of the road. He slowed and pointed it out to Suk Hing. She quickly jumped off the bike and went to retrieve it.

"Hey, it's a ten yuan note!" she exclaimed, returning to Bui and handing it over. "You should keep it, you never know, we might need it for something."

"Are you sure?"

"Yes, take it, you were the one who spotted it."

Bui took the note and tucked it safely into the pocket of his pants. Feeling like it might be a good omen, Suk Hing jumped back on the bike and they continued their ride. It was nearly seven p.m. when Bui decided it was dark and quiet enough on the streets for them to safely approach his house. Suk Hing was ushered inside and once more greeted warmly by the family she remembered: the mother, the younger brother, and the sister who had become a dear friend in the short time she had spent sharing her room.

There wasn't the opportunity for too many pleasantries this time, though; things were much more dangerous. Suk Hing knew the house wasn't as safe as before since Bui was, like her, now under the watchful eye of the government. She was escorted to the attic, where she was to stay until everything was in place. Bui needed to spend a day or two carrying out his usual routine, allowing any suspicion of his trip into the city to pass. He also needed to put the final preparations in place for their departure.

Suk Hing passed that night and the following day mostly in solitude in the attic. Hot meals were brought to her and a few words were exchanged in hushed tones, but the family member making the delivery could never linger, as the house could be searched at any time. It was a lonely time. Her mind roamed back over all the people who had been involved in her life, the good and the bad, which came around full circle to Bui and his family. They were showing a great deal of bravery and defiance by having her there. Bui was already a marked traitor and now they were harbouring a known fugitive. She didn't know what Bui's daily tasks were, but she knew they would be arduous and unsavoury, designed to humiliate and punish him. She knew she should be grateful for the rare chance to rest and build up her strength for the journey to come, and she was, but she was also restless in the confined and lonely attic.

She tried to sleep as much as she could but she was constantly woken by the announcements bursting from the speakers outside. No matter where she had travelled, she hadn't been able to escape the propaganda that tried to worm its way into her head. Every village, every town, every city and even the large ferries had speakers playing the same voice reading the same speeches. With nothing to help her block out the sound in the quiet loft, she was forced to listen.

"Mao Zedong's thought is the guiding principle for all the work of the Party, the army, and the country!"

Suk Hing snorted. All she knew was that it was the guiding principle for hundreds of people to tear themselves away from their family and friends and risk everything to flee their own country. She covered her ears and tried to ignore the voice.

The monotony was broken on the second night when Bui brought someone to meet her. He was a short, stocky, strong-looking man around twenty-four years old, the complete opposite of Bui physically, who was tall and skinny. Bui introduced him as Lum Jong Qwan, and explained that he was going to join them on their escape attempt. Suk Hing introduced herself and they chatted for a while, getting to know each other. He had a very different dialect than she was used to, and she found it hard to understand what he was saying at first. He seemed pleasant enough and Suk Hing liked him, although he didn't offer much in the way of small talk. It was Bui who explained that they were long-time friends, and that Lum Jong would be a great asset to them because he had lived in the area they needed to travel to for a long time. He knew the terrain and could plan a route that would give them the best, and safest, chance to escape. Lum Jong told them that as they got closer to the ocean there were three borders they would need to cross.

"The first," he explained, "has a small village within its boundaries. Although it is guarded, people are allowed to come and go provided they are visiting someone who lives there. If you are stopped, you will be asked to provide a name and address."

"Do you actually know someone who lives there? Do we have a name and address we can use?" Suk Hing asked.

"No, I don't."

"So what are we going to do?"

"I think our best bet would be to try and find a way around the village; see if there is any cover when we get there that we can move through."

"Okay," Suk Hing said. It wasn't much of a plan, but it was the best they had at the moment. "What next?"

"After that village there is a long hike, and at the end of that walk there is another village. This one is a lot trickier as it is closer to the shore. The only way you can enter it is to have a valid certificate stating your right to be in the area. Villagers have to obtain this certificate before they leave the area to collect supplies, and are only allowed back in if they show it on their return.

"The third border is the worst. There aren't any villages and residents, and no farms. It's an empty military zone that is entirely off-limits to any civilians. It's well patrolled and so close to the water's edge that there is only one reason for people to be there – and the soldiers know it."

"Suk Hing," Bui interrupted. "I believe this is where you actually tried to make it to the water the first time. Can you describe it for us?"

Suk Hing described the terrain, the guards' movements, the dogs, and how she had managed to make it to the shore on her first attempt

"Yes, that sounds like what I have heard," Lum Jong said.

They talked on, but could come to no firm decisions on how best to handle things that night. The only thing they settled on was that they would always try to travel at night, when they could hope to pass by any towns or dwellings unnoticed. After Bui and Lum Jong left, Suk Hing tried to sleep, but her mind was full of the information she had been given, and trying to work out ways to deal with it. Without actually knowing the area, she couldn't plan with any conviction. As the night wore on, her doubts only grew.

Chapter Fourteen

"Control your emotions or they will control you"

September 1ˢᵗ, 1966: 4 AM

Suk Hing spent the next day gathering her strength and forcing the mounting worries from her mind, mentally preparing herself for the journey, which was to begin the following morning. When the morning arrived, she was ready. As before, she would carry with her the deflated soccer ball bladders, but Bui's family had also provided a twenty-five foot rope, which could be useful given the mountainous terrain. More than this, though, Suk Hing was ready to face whatever adversity arose with determination, and would let nothing stand in her way. This was her last shot, and if it didn't work she would die trying rather than rot in jail for the rest of her days.

She and Bui were having one last meal when Lum Jong arrived at the house at half-past four in the afternoon. He had already eaten so declined the invitation to join them. Before it was time to leave, Suk Hing once again left any money she had with Bui's mother and they parted with tears in their eyes and wishes of good luck. Like last time, they left on bikes driven by family members. Lum Jong and Bui rode with their respective brothers, while Suk Hing travelled with Bui's sister. They left shortly after dinner; Suk Hing estimated the time to be around six p.m.

As they cycled along secluded gravel trails and winding back roads and the mountains rose nebulously on either side of the anxious travellers, Suk Hing began to lose her bearings. Within the mounting gloom, she could no longer track the direction in they were moving, or for how long they had been travelling. Bui's brother and sister cycled side by side, so she could just make out Bui in the dark. When a sliver of moonlight managed to creep over the shadow of the mountains Suk Hing could see that he was trembling. Her heart sank; if Bui was this terrified already, it was possible that he could be a real liability on the journey ahead. He had to toughen up if he was to survive this. She was the only one who had made it as far as the water before. She knew exactly how panic and fear could overtake you in the icy darkness. If he panicked, there was little hope of survival.

"Any idea what time it is?" she asked him, hoping to distract him from whatever fears were running through his mind.

He glanced at her then pulled out an ornate pocket watch, opening it up to squint at the face in the half-light.

"That's a pretty watch."

"Yes, it's a family heirloom. It's about nine-thirty p.m."

They had been cycling for three and a half hours. She didn't ask Bui what he was going to do with watch when they reached the water; he seemed worried enough already.

Half an hour later, Lum Jong indicated they were approaching the departure point and that they should be ready to jump. Still disoriented from the sinuous mountain paths, Suk Hing had no idea how Lum Jong knew where they were, but she tensed herself for the imminent leap regardless. The bikes slowed a little and the three sprung off, running to the bushes at the side of the road and taking cover there. They watched the bikes immediately turn round and head back in the direction they had come, none of the cyclists even glancing at the bushes as they passed. They lay there in silence, waiting for about ten minutes to ensure everything was quiet, and giving the cyclists enough time to get out of the area. Once they were certain nothing was amiss and they'd had time to get their bearings, the three cautiously emerged from their cover and began to walk in single file along the edge of the road.

They hadn't been walking long when a sound reached Bui's ears and he stopped dead in his tracks.

"Someone's coming," he hissed. "Hide!"

The three dived back into the bushes, and listened hard to the night, but nothing stirred. They crept back out to the road and continued on. The walk along the shadowy road was already tense, but Bui's jumpiness had seemed to infect them all, and several more times they had to scramble for cover when one of them thought they heard someone approaching. Each time it turned out to be nothing and they would cautiously re-emerge to continue on, feeling a little foolish.

They walked that way for two hours, the tension causing their muscles to ache. Bui and Suk Hing both jumped when Lum Jong suddenly held out a hand to halt them.

"We're coming up to the first border," he hissed to them. "We have to go around the village."

Suk Hing stared into the darkness ahead. She couldn't see any lights or other signs to indicate that they were coming upon a settlement, but she put her doubts aside and trusted Lum Jong. After all, he was the one who supposedly knew the area and he seemed confident of their whereabouts. He moved off to the left and Suk Hing and Bui followed blindly. They were moving stealthily through the bushes when the sound of laughter reached their ears.

Suk Hing stopped and listened carefully. It sounded like a large group of children playing. The three of them held position, waiting and hoping that the children would pass by. As the voices and laughter grew louder, they realized that the children were heading in their direction, and they were right in their path. If the children spotted them, there was no doubt they would call out and perhaps fetch an adult. The three of them looked at each other, the same anxiety reflected back at them from each face. They nodded to each other and scrambled, searching for better cover away from the path of the advancing group.

Suk Hing grabbed Bui and pulled her with him, knowing that his fear meant he was the greatest danger to them all. In the rapidly fading twilight, Suk Hing glimpsed a small ditch at the side of the road, which looked to be about three or four foot deep. It was their best shot. She jumped in and pulled Bui with her. Her feet splashed into ankle-deep water and Suk Hing held her breath, wondering if the sound would have been heard over the voices of the children. She couldn't hear any cries of surprise, only muffled chatter. A noise above startled her, but as she peered over the top of the ditch, she realized it was only Lum Jong trying to find a place to hide. Suk Hing watched as he lay on the ground, covering himself in the leaves of a sweet potato bush that grew along the edge of the ditch.

As they all went silent, Suk Hing realized she could hear the water lapping and splashing nearby. She whirled round to locate the source of the noise, exasperated when she found it was Bui; he was shaking so violently in that few inches of ditch water in which he crouched was undulating and splashing against him. She scolded him, quietly telling him they were only children and to pull himself together. She gripped him firmly, trying to hold him steady, not really comfortable with touching him but having no choice.

"It's probably just kids being let out from a night school, Bui, stop it. They won't see us, but if you don't calm down, they might hear us."

Bui did his best to relax his muscles, but it still took most of Suk Hing's strength to keep him as steady as possible. Finally, the voices moved away, and the night was quiet once more, save for the tiny rustlings and distant calls of nocturnal animals. Suk Hing climbed from the ditch and pulled Bui out after her. She made her way over to Lum Jong and helped him remove the spade-shaped sweet potato leaves as quietly as possible. Once they were all on their feet they resumed their journey, making a large circle around the village. It added distance and time to their journey, but it was their only option. Suk Hing had to tread lightly, her wet shoes making a squelching sound as she walked. She hoped they would dry soon, as it was adding to the discomfort of the long walk.

Soon the terrain changed. Having reached the foot of the first mountain, the party found themselves traversing a steep incline. As they climbed, the path beneath their feet became rockier and more uneven, the loose stones underfoot posing new dangers. Suk Hing was glad of the moonlight, its bare silver gleam offering slight but necessary guidance as the trail narrowed and all but dissolved among spills of limestone slag. They climbed single file throughout the night.

Around six a.m., the sun began to rise, and the party greeted the dim red glow emanating from behind the mountaintops with mixed feelings. The high altitude meant it was very windy and they were freezing, and the constant movement was the only thing that had kept their body temperatures at safe levels during the long, dark hours. They each welcomed the coming heat, but not its light, for while the sun would provide much-needed warmth, its arrival also meant that they would be highly visible. There was practically no cover this far up, the sparse vegetation limited to the odd clump of scrub and the occasional gaunt tree. In the dawn's emergent light the surrounding area looked barren and hostile.

"We need to find somewhere to hide and to rest while we can."

The two boys agreed, and they began their search before the sun had fully risen. Suk Hing found a cavity welled into the side of the mountain, around six feet wide by eight feet long, and approximately four feet deep. She shivered as she looked into it. It looked man-made and made her think of a grave. She dismissed the possibility of hiding in such a place as far too disturbing, but after searching for another ten minutes and finding nothing, she had to concede that there was little choice. She pointed it out to the boys and they congratulated her on her find, not seeing what she saw as she stared back into the condensed void of the grave-shaped trench. They jumped in without hesitation and Suk Hing had no choice but to follow. She reluctantly jumped in, her skin crawling.

Once they had determined they could all fit comfortably, they climbed out again and broke some of the tiny, one-foot high trees, carrying them over to the hole. Once back inside, they used the trees to cover themselves, hoping they would provide enough seclusion no matter what occurred through the daylight hours. They decided one should stay awake to act as a lookout while the others slept, so Suk Hing volunteered to take the first shift.

Lying awake, listening out while the boys slept, her imagination began to run wild. Being all but entombed in the grave-like hole felt like an omen, and Suk Hing wondered if this mountain would be the place of her demise. Would she be spotted by soldiers, shot on the spot? Would she die from exposure or lack of food, or would she slip and fall on the mountain, injuring herself so badly she couldn't continue, forcing the others to leave her behind to her fate, ending up food for some ravenous mountain bird or beast of prey? Feeling the panic caused by the rising claustrophobia, Suk Hing gave herself a firm mental shake. She couldn't let any of that happen. She just had to make it. She tried to turn her thoughts to happier times as she left the boys to sleep for as long as she could. As she began to feel her head grow heavy and her eyelids begin to droop, she woke Bui to take the next watch, curling up into a ball and hoping she didn't have nightmares as she slept.

She was awoken just as the sun began to set. The orange glow was fading fast from the sky, and the three watched in silence until it had disappeared completely below the horizon. In the dusk, they freed themselves from the trees and climbed out of their hiding place. Suk Hing had never been so relieved and was anxious to start walking, putting the horrible thoughts created by the hideous space far behind her. In the moonlight they managed to hit upon the trail, and they followed this through the night, climbing and descending as they followed the rise and fall of the mountain range. She had no idea how far they had travelled, or how many villages nestled in the foothills they had passed, moving like ghosts in the night high above them as the residents slept peacefully in their beds, warm under the covers.

Suddenly, something caught Suk Hing's eye to her left. She slowly turned her head, almost afraid to look. She could make out a tiny amber glow in the darkness, which would occasionally flare brighter. She caught the other's arms, indicating they should stop and be silent. Staring intently in the direction of the light, she willed her eyes to adjust until she could make out the shape of a man in the moonlight. It looked like he was lying on his back, staring up at the night sky as he smoked a cigarette. They were close enough that she could smell the tobacco smoke. The three looked at each other with panic in their eyes. She kept a tight hold of Bui, afraid he would flee, making enough noise to alert the man. There wasn't much reason for anybody to be this high up in the mountains at this time. He might be like them, but if he was, he was being very careless with the cigarette being so easily visible. Suk Hing thought the only explanation was that he was a soldier patrolling the mountaintop, perhaps taking a break, perhaps not really expecting to encounter anyone in this lonely duty. If he was a soldier, he obviously hadn't spotted them or he would have reacted by now.

"I think he's a soldier," she murmured to the others.

"You're not allowed to smoke in the army," Bui whispered back. "Maybe he's just some random guy."

"Random or not, he's a danger to us. Let's hope he is a soldier who isn't supposed to be smoking, it might give us something to bargain with if we have to, but we'd be better shutting up and trying to sneak past without him seeing us."

Suk Hing motioned for them to move forward. They crept away as slowly and stealthily as they could, hoping the man was too lost in his thoughts to be paying much attention to his surroundings. They moved their feet carefully, trying not to dislodge any loose stones that might skitter and clatter across the path.

A grassy expanse appeared to Suk Hing's right, the naturally occurring meadow materializing before them like a desert oasis within the barren mountain waste. They made for it, moving faster and more confidently as the ground underfoot softened. They lay down at the edge of the field, hoping the man would eventually move off in the opposite direction. They waited for some time, but heard and saw nothing. Perhaps he was a stationary guard, assigned to that particular area, or maybe he was too lazy to carry out his duties the way he was supposed to. Suk Hing and Lum Jong shared a silent look: they couldn't lie here and waste the entire night. They had to take a chance, and move.

The two of them rose and motioned to Bui to follow, hoping they had come far enough beyond the man that they were out of his vision and hearing, even if he hadn't moved off. He might have come in this direction, but they couldn't hear anything so had to assume he was still in the same place or had gone the other way. Bui was shaking so much he could barely stand, let alone walk. In the moonlight his face had taken an ashen cast. His eyes, dark and wide as jet saucers, radiated with uncontained panic. He looked at Suk Hing pleadingly, and she understood that he was having serious second thoughts. As she helped him to his feet and gave him a shoulder to lean on until his rubbery legs could move, she wondered how far he had made it the first time he had tried, and how he had screwed up enough courage to even make the attempt in the first place. She knew that he was brave as he had helped shelter her the first time and had taken her to the mountains, and he had survived his time in prison and whatever humiliation the government had heaped upon him. She had to consider that perhaps Bui knew more of what happened to second-time escapees when they were caught than she did. It was the only thing that could account for his lack of courage now. She didn't dare probe him; it was better not to know. With Lum Jong supporting Bui from the other side, they managed to move back onto the trail. Bui's anxiety subsided as they further they moved from the area, and after a short time he was once again able to walk on his own.

It was just as well, as they soon reached another incline, steep and treacherous.

"Perhaps we should go around, this looks too difficult to climb without any equipment," Bui suggested.
 "Going around would take us at least six hours," Lum Jong replied. "Going up and along will be much faster. Besides, if we go around we'll be too close to the villages in the valleys. I don't think we have any option but to climb and hope for the best."

It was more of a scramble than a climb as they tried to navigate the rocky mountainside. Suk Hing slipped several times, managing to find handholds to cling to until she had regained her footing. After climbing for what felt like hours, Suk Hing finally crested a broad mesa. She didn't know how the other two had fared on the climb as she had been too intent on not falling to notice, but they were both with her as she straightened up on the apex, relieved they had each managed to survive the ordeal. They moved on, following a narrow spoor across the plateau in the dark, and paying no heed to their throbbing feet and aching legs.

"I think we should stop for the night," Lum Jong said. "If we carry on, we will arrive close to the third border in the daylight. We want to avoid that at all costs. We won't make it in time tonight so we should stop here, then move tomorrow night while we have hours of darkness left. Besides, there is always a shift change at seven a.m. and that's when most of the army will be moving about and walking to different points. We should hide before that begins. Since we have Bui's watch we can keep an eye on the time as we hunt for a good place."

It seemed like a sensible suggestion and Suk Hing knew she would be glad of the rest after the gruelling climb. The three began to search for a good hiding spot to keep them safe through the day. It wasn't long before Bui discovered a strange-looking bore in the mountainside, just large enough for someone to crawl through. Bui didn't dare investigate the inside on his own.

"I'll go," Suk Hing volunteered.

"No, I'll go," Lum Jong said. "I'm the one that might not fit, so I might as well find out, as well as see what's inside."

Suk Hing waited anxiously with Bui as Lum Jong tried to wedge his stocky body through the narrow mouth of the burrow. Bui clutched her hand as Lum Jong disappeared from view. Once again, she felt uncomfortable with the intimacy, but under the circumstances she decided to allow it. They both breathed a sigh of relief as Lum Jong's face appeared back at the entrance.

"Must be a den of some sort, but nobody's home," he said, his joke falling flat. "I don't think anything has lived in here for a while so it should be safe enough. I think we'll all fit, although it's going to be tight. It's probably the best we're going to find."

"Okay then, Bui, you go next."

He made his way into the hole, happy now that they were taking cover. Suk Hing followed. "Tight" had been an understatement. There wasn't enough headroom to properly sit, and the interior wasn't wide enough for the three of them to lie down except in the fetal position, on their sides with their heads bent down and their knees tucked tightly up to their chests. It was comfortable enough for the first half hour, but after that, they all longed to be able to stretch out as well as escape the lingering musk of whatever derelict mountain fox or cat once sheltered there. However, they were safe and secluded, and could rest without worry of being discovered. They forced themselves to lie there until they all fell asleep.

They awoke several times throughout the day, but didn't dare break cover to stretch their limbs. They could hear the dull whir of planes passing overhead, probably air patrols to watch the mountains, adding to the efficiency of the foot soldiers. Huddled and rigid, they stayed within, hoping to be able to go back to sleep until finally twilight arrived.

Dusk was as welcome as the dawn had been the morning before. Cramps and aches tore through Suk Hing's body as she scrabbled back through the cave mouth and onto mountainside. The others, equally atrophied from the day-long sequester, crawled painfully out after her. The three of them lay there on the ground vigorously massaging their arms and legs, trying to get their bodies to comply. It took almost an hour before the cramps in their limbs would subside and their muscles would move fluidly enough that they could resume their journey.

They walked for another two hours or so, Suk Hing experiencing threatening twinges and jerks in several muscles, but the cramps stayed at bay, allowing her to keep up a brisk pace. The trail took them to the very edge of a precipice. Standing precariously at the edge of the cliff face, Suk Hing peered into the near dark and caught a familiar sight. Far below stretched a grassy plain approximately three-hundred meters in length. The vegetation had been cut down, so the expanse was nearly bare. To the east, the sea crashed in a regular rhythm of breaking waves. Despite not having a plan, despite not having any sense of distance and direction, despite placing her trust in a man she barely knew, Suk Hing had once again reached the third, and most dangerous, border.

Chapter Fifteen

"Today's task, today's job to complete."

September 4^{th,} 1966: 10 PM

The three refugees huddled on the mountaintop, surveying the drop below. The descent, sheer and unforgiving, was going to be difficult. The long walks had already worn down Suk Hing's shoes, and the previous day's climb had ruined them completely. The spares she had replaced them with were now equally threadbare, the soles thin and smooth, making them slippery. She wondered if she might be better off attempting the descent barefoot, but the mountainside was barbed with shale outcroppings, edged like knives. What little protection her shoes could still afford would be better than no protection at all; she would just have to be aware that her feet could give way at any moment, and try her best to compensate. They were so close: plunging to their deaths from the clifftop was not an option.

They studied the cliff face in silence, their minds trying to plot a route along the mountain's vertiginous, geologically plotless, decline. It looked absolutely terrifying, their most difficult challenge yet, even without the soldiers positioned at various points along the base below. Suk Hing thought back to her days in the park, meeting with other like-minded people who all planned to make the trip. Her mind drifted over each one, wondering how they had fared and whether they too had arrived at this very spot, trying to work out how to make the descent without falling to their deaths, just as she was now. She wondered if there might be bodies, twisted and broken and forgotten in the crevices, or lying prone among the sea-lyme grass dotting the plain below. Then, she recalled something else, a piece of information she had heard during one of the meetings.

"Someone once said that the patrols only move every four hours, but I'm not sure whether to believe that. It seems an awful long time for a place they know to be a high-risk area," she whispered to the others. "Maybe they rely on the soldiers positioned in the mountains and the spotters in the planes, and if nobody has reported anything then maybe they feel secure in the fact that no one is suddenly going to appear here," Bui stated.

"They wouldn't take that kind of chance; I just don't trust that information. I think we should wait for a while and keep an eye on them. We can use Bui's watch to time their movements."

The others agreed. They checked the time and settled in for a long wait on the cold, hard ground. It didn't take long for Suk Hing to begin shivering, and she had to set her jaw to stop her teeth from chattering. They waited there in the dark, doing their version of reconnaissance on the soldiers below. Her mind began to recollect the journey, all that they had been through, and how far they had come. It seemed cruel that people could have made it this far only to fall, get caught, or drown. Suk Hing wondered if the eyes of the world were watching China, if they knew of the adversity the people faced, of the bravery of those who tried to escape. Perhaps the government were covering it up, playing down the situation, but surely those in Hong Kong would know. She had no idea what happened to people who reached the other side, but whatever awaited her there it couldn't be worse than her life here.

Suk Hing's reflections were broken by a fleck of white light moving below and to the right. The soldiers were moving. Bui checked his watch: two hours had passed.

"It looks like they carry out patrols every two hours, not four."

They watched as the beam from the soldier's flashlight below them jerked and bobbed from right to left, sweeping the area.

"Definitely a patrol," Lum Jong said. "We should get moving just as they pass directly below us. I don't think they'll hear us when we're this far up, and by the time we get lower, they'll be well on their way. That gives us the maximum time to get down, or to maybe get away if we fall and are still alive."

"What if there's a second patrol moving from left to right, like a relay? We'll be sitting ducks stuck halfway down if that's the case," Suk Hing argued. "Or maybe they get so far along and turn and come right back."

"All the more reason to move now and get down as far as we can, as fast as we can. Last time you got down and ran and that didn't work. This time, we should get down and hide down there, timing our run better. There must be somewhere to hide closer to the bottom. We don't have to go all the way to the plain, just far enough until it isn't so steep and we're much nearer to where we need to be."

Suk Hing wasn't convinced that this was the best plan, but she couldn't deny that her last attempt had failed. Even Lum Jong and Bui didn't know that she had actually made it to the water; she had never told a single soul. With Bui as nervous as he was, this wasn't the time to share that information with them. There was also a small part of her that was glad to have someone else strong around, someone else to make some of the decisions and take control now and again. She decided that she would follow the plan. The more time they spent discussing it the more time they wasted, and another patrol could already be on their way.

The three took a deep breath, shared a look, and began the treacherous descent. Suk Hing was torn between taking it slow, aware both of the inadequate grips on her shoes and the risk of falling, and hurrying down so they had time to hide if they made it to the bottom. Lum Jong had taken the lead, with Suk Hing following and Bui at the rear. As Lum Jong began to move, Suk Hing realized that the question of whether to take the descent slowly or quickly was largely moot. She had to follow the pace set by Lum Jong or Bui might get too close, having to stop behind her. Downward momentum would help them maintain their balance, so stopping wasn't an option for any of them. She just hoped that Bui could handle this; if he fell, he would likely take them all with him on his way down.

Suk Hing had never been as scared in her life as she was during that time, not even when she awoke on the beach to find herself under a halo of gun barrels. There were no trails, no set routes. She could hardly see a thing and had to blindly follow Lum Jong's lead, hoping that she could emulate his movements as he struggled to find toeholds and places to grip as he went. She wasn't as strong as he was, and neither was Bui. She hoped he took that into consideration as he led them on their way.

Eventually, Suk Hing felt the ground beneath her shift, as the cliffside's near perpendicular incline evened slightly into a steep but less hazardous slope. She stopped and looked around for potential hiding places. A few thickets of trees dotted the escarpment, but they didn't extend very far. She waited for Bui to reach her, thinking this would be the best place to find a hiding spot while they tried to time their run. In the hiatus, Suk Hing had lost sight of Lum Jong. She looked into the near distance, but couldn't see him anywhere; darkness cloaked the landscape like a shroud. She dared not call out, so she took Bui's arm and moved further down towards the base of the mountain, assuming that Lum Jong had carried on further down. As Suk Hing's eyes readjusted in the gloom, she spotted Lum crouched just past the edge of a tree line about twenty yards in front of her.

Beyond, the slope became gentler and then flattened out, stretching into the large expanse of exposed area that they had seen clearly from their perch on the cliff face earlier.

As they stood together staring out over the road separating them from the patrol area, Suk Hing couldn't believe that they had all made it safely down. Her heart was pounding and her breathing was ragged, but she was alive and, for the moment, in one piece. It seemed like a miracle, one she hadn't believed possible when she had first turned her back on the cliff edge and took that first step down into the empty, black expanse.

Her relief was short-lived. The telltale beam of a flashlight was moving in their direction. It was much larger and brighter than the pinprick they had made out from the top of the mountain. She gestured to the others.

"Hide!," Lum Jong said, and they moved without hesitation. Suk Hing grasped Bui by the arm, pulling him alongside her in case he froze. She found a large rock and looked around anxiously as she ushered Bui behind it, following only once she was certain he was hidden from the view of the approaching patrol. The two of them huddled there together, hoping that the dogs wouldn't catch their scents, and hoping that Lum Jong had also found cover. Suk Hing wanted to call for him, to ensure he was all right, but it would have been suicide. Forcing her voice back into her throat, Suk Hing instead focused her attentions on Bui, on ensuring that he didn't panic and flee crashing through the trees, giving away their position.

After a while, she plucked up the courage to peek over the top of the rock. She couldn't see any light at all, not even the retreating glow of the flashlight. The patrol must have passed by. Lum Jong must have been safe. Suk Hing stood up slowly and motioned for Bui to follow. They crept quietly to the other side of the rock. Suk Hing tried to remember the direction in which Lum Jong had moved after he'd told them to hide.

She searched behind nearby rocks and checked the surrounding trees to see if Lum Jong had climbed up into them to stay out of sight. She tried to move as quickly and quietly as possible, Bui close on her heels. There was no trace of Lum Jong, or any sign that someone had passed this way. The surrounding vegetation appeared undisturbed. Suk Hing thought that she may have travelled in the wrong direction, doubling back and moving in a zigzag pattern in case she had missed him first time round.

She and Bui moved some distance in the other direction, but they still couldn't find Lum. They navigated their way back to their original hiding place behind the large rock, using it as a point of reference. They worked their way back up the slope in case he had retreated further up the mountain, but they found nothing. Lum Jong seemed to have vanished.

On their way back to the rock, Suk Hing spotted another beam of light. She couldn't be certain, but it seemed like the patrols were circulating every ten minutes, not every two hours, as they had initially thought. The current patrol was again coming from their right. Suk Hing deduced that a constant stream of patrols would be making their way back and forth in front of them. Perhaps other spotters had seen something suspicious and alerted the soldiers here to be on their guard. As the light approached, Suk Hing once again pulled Bui into hiding. He was shaking badly; the frequency and proximity of the soldiers were clearly terrifying him. After a few interminable minutes, Suk Hing stuck her head out of hiding and looked around. She couldn't see the light anymore but it worried her that it had disappeared so quickly. Had the soldiers taken a different route, maybe moving off their regular path because something had caught their attention? If that was the case, they could appear anywhere at any moment. Suk Hing knew she had to make a decision.

"Bui, we have to go. *Now.*"

"No! We can't leave Lum Jong."

"We've looked in every direction except forward, maybe he's already gone. Have you thought of that?"

"He wouldn't leave me," Bui said, almost pleading.

"He knew you were with me, and he knew I would make the decision to go. We've done all we can. We're not trackers, but we can't even see a place where he might have hidden. We could be here for hours looking and never find him. By then it will be daylight. Is that what you would prefer? Because if it is, you might as well step out there and give yourself up right now."

Suk Hing knew she was being harsh, but it was the only way she could make Bui pull himself together and think logically. She wanted him to survive this; she wanted him to be free.

"Please, Bui," she said, changing tactics. "We can't stay here any longer; it's getting more and more dangerous by the second. We've wasted enough time looking and put ourselves at risk in doing so. Either Lum Jong has gone already, or he will understand why we decided to go. Maybe he'll even catch up. He's fast and he's strong, right?"

Bui simply nodded, looking pale and miserable.

"Right, so we have to go now. Come on, please. We need to move."

"I don't want to go without Lum Jong. I've never mentioned this, but I'm not a very good swimmer. He was supposed to help me in the water. Suk Hing, without his strength, I'll never make it. I know you worked as a life-guard, but you couldn't support me all the way, not for eight hours solid and fighting against waves and currents."

Suk Hing hung her head. As much as she would like to think she might be able to help Bui swim, she knew in her heart that he was right. She was an expert swimmer, yet even she had been exhausted after the swim the last time, and hadn't had the strength left to fight the ebbing tide. There was no way she could make it if she had to pull Bui along with her.

"Okay, then," she said sadly. "Then these are your choices. You can come with me, hoping we make it across the highway and find him already there, and maybe even spot him in the water. Once we get far enough out, he might even wait for us to catch up with him. If we don't find him, you have to swim; you have to believe you can do it. I do."

"I don't think I can, not without Lum Jong. The water scares me too much."

"Then the only other choice is to turn back now. I'm sorry Bui, but it would be the safest option. Once we're at the other side of the road, there is no turning back and no time to hesitate. At least from here, you have a chance. I'll go on by myself, and once I hit the water, or if the soldiers spot me and give chase, you grab the opportunity while they're distracted. Get yourself back up that mountain and follow the trail home. Do what we did on the way here, travel at night and hide during the daylight hours. You'll find your way."

"I don't know what to do; I don't want to go back to that life."

"It's time to make up your mind, Bui, because I'm going while I still can."

Without another word, Suk Hing turned and ran.

Chapter Sixteen

"To sail the boat against the current"

September 4ᵗʰ, 1966: 10:30 PM

She ran for all she was worth, pumping her arms and legs in a full-out sprint, making it across the highway and reaching the barren flatlands. She didn't look around or behind her. It didn't matter if soldiers were standing only a few feet away, or even surrounding her, she could not, and would not, stop now. She just had to keep moving as fast as she possibly could. She focused completely on her destination: the beach at the end of the long stretch of exposed ground.

Suk Hing was overjoyed when she heard running foot-steps and breathing close behind her. She instinctively knew that it was Bui, and was more than relieved that he had decided to follow. She'd had a feeling that he would come to his senses once left behind on his own. It had been a risky move on her part as she didn't want to abandon him, but she'd had no choice. She had to trust her instincts and force his hand. If she hadn't, he would have hesitated and argued with her all night.

As she ran on, another sound filled her with joy. She could faintly hear the ocean, and with every few seconds, it seemed to be getting that little bit louder. As Suk Hing reached the end of the plain, a four-foot drop suddenly opened before her. She barely broke stride as she leapt down and landed on the sandy beach below. A soft thud behind her indicated that Bui had followed. In seconds, both of them had scrambled back to their feet and continued to run. It was hard going through the soft, shifting sand, but they managed to maintain a decent pace through sheer willpower alone, pushing their bodies as hard as they could. Despite their efforts, it still felt as if they were moving in slow motion.

Suddenly, the ground firmed up beneath them. Momentum carried them across the hard, wet sand, finally depositing them at the water's edge. They crouched there, badly winded and gasping for breath. The night was clear and bright with stars. They stayed low, obscure shapes not easily discernible from a distance.

Suk Hing couldn't believe she had made it this far a second time, but she also knew that they were still far from safe. She couldn't see any jostling beams of light in the distance, nor did she hear any barking from the dogs or shouting from the soldiers, but they could still be spotted here. There wasn't much time.

"Where is it?!?," Bui suddenly hissed, breaking the silence. "Oh, no! Where did it go?!!" He was hunting frantically around his clothing, checking every pocket. He had dropped to his knees, but his back was straight, probably a recognizable shape.

"What? What is it?," Suk Hing replied, alarmed.

"I can't find the Hong Kong ten yuan note,"

"Forget about it, it doesn't matter. Stay low."

"It does matter; we're going to need it."

He continued to search, ignoring Suk Hing as she scurried round to his backpack and retrieved his two soccer ball bladders and a makeshift net bag. Despite still being breathless from the run, she began inflating one of the bladders. It was much harder than she expected. No matter how deep a breath she took and how hard she blew, the thick, flattened rubber of the bladder barely seemed to move. Finally, there was a slight movement in the material, and it spurred her on. By the time Suk Hing had managed to inflate the first bladder, her lungs were burning and she felt light headed, but she moved straight to the next.

"I found it!" Bui declared triumphantly, as if everything rested on him finding that note. "It was in the pocket of my pants all along."

Suk Hing merely nodded, her lips pressed firmly against the ball. She waved for him to get back down and he complied, happy now that he had found what he was frantically searching for. Once she had the second makeshift float ready, she packed them both into the netted bag and tied the net around Bui's chest. She adjusted the floats slightly so that they sat on his back at either side, positioned close to his armpits. Satisfied with her work, she decided not to blow up her own bladders just yet. Her chest still hurt and she was dizzy, besides, they had spent long enough hanging around this beach. Even one more minute could be too long. She would blow up her own floats once they were in the water.

"Time to go, you're all set," she told Bui.

He hesitated, looking at the breaking waves with trepidation. He began to tremble again, from cold or fear, or perhaps both.

"I'm scared, Suk Hing."

Relying on the tactic that had worked last time, Suk Hing was all business. "I'm not waiting for you, you're coming with me."

She grabbed Bui with her left hand and dragged him into the water. The water felt slightly cold, but they were chilled to the bone anyway after travelling for several nights at high altitude so it didn't feel so bad to them. Keeping tight hold of Bui, Suk Hing moved through the water, easily at first, then with more exaggerated, large steps as it came higher up her thighs, then her waist, then her chest. She estimated that they had managed to walk about one hundred yards before her feet lost contact with the ground below. She stopped there and let go of Bui, allowing him to float with the rubber aids. Once she was certain he was fine, she attempted to remove her backpack from her shoulders.

As she struggled, she kept an eye on the waves. A large one was approaching fast, so she abandoned her fight with her pack and ducked under the surface, allowing it to pass safely overhead. She popped back up a few seconds later, horrified to see Bui being pushed back to the shoreline by the tide. He was already half way there.

Without hesitation, she made her way back to him, grabbing hold of him before he got any closer to the beach.

"What are you doing?," she hissed.

"I don't know," he cried. "I told you I can't swim."

"You're supposed to go under the waves, okay?"

Bui didn't acknowledge her; he was pale and shaking, his eyes glassy as if he was in shock. Suk Hing wondered if he had ever been in the water before, and was beginning to suspect he hadn't. This was worse than she thought.

"Well, now you know, right? We have to move; the dogs could still spot us or hear us. We're too close to shore, if they see us, they would catch up to us in no time."

She grabbed Bui once more and dragged him back to the point where her feet could no longer touch the sea-bed. She let go, but stayed closer to him this time. She couldn't deny how worried she was. Bui had been like a rag doll, limp and floppy in the water, forcing her to do all the work of dragging him along despite the fact that he could have walked. She could understand now why he had been reluctant to carry on without Lum Jong. Bui had probably planned to rely on his friend dragging him the entire way.

She lifted one leg up as high as she could and crunched her body in the middle, reaching her feet so she could take off her shoes. They would hamper her during the swim, but she needed to hang onto them. The coral reefs were rough and might hurt her feet; far more dangerous, though, were the razor-sharp oyster beds. She risked cutting her feet to ribbons if she came across one without protection. She had just freed her foot from the second shoe when another incoming wave forced her beneath the water's surface again. She had no time to grab Bui, but hoped he had followed her instructions. No such luck. When she emerged, there was no sign of him, until she looked back towards the shoreline and spotted him nearly back on the beach yet again.

"Stupid, stupid, stupid!," she hissed in a half whisper, slapping the water hard in frustration. She tucked her shoes into the waistband of her pants and swam halfway back towards Bui, motioning for him to come back out and join her. He stood still, staring at her. She motioned again, and this time, he started to move, very slowly half-walking and half-swimming in her direction.

This is ridiculous, she thought. *We're going to be here all night, going back and forth in this same few feet of water, still here like sitting ducks when the sun rises, a nice game for the dogs and target practice for the soldiers.*

Finally, Bui came within arm's length of her and she reached out and grabbed him, pulling him out the rest of the way.

"When I tell you to duck your head, you do it!" she yelled at him, too frustrated to care if her voice carried back to the patrols on land.

Bui just stared, showing no sign he had understood or even heard her. He looked exhausted and defeated. She was almost tempted to alert the soldiers; maybe the dogs snapping at his heels would bring him out of his daze and get him moving. Shaking her head, she moved to the rear

188

of him, grabbing the netting tightly with her right hand, just below the back of his neck. Positioning herself slightly to his left, she stretched out her left arm, lifted her legs, and began kicking. It wasn't easy — her inability to use both of her arms to swim meant that she would be using more energy and moving slower —, but she was able to push Bui through the water, making at least some progress and getting further from the shore than they had been before. As a large breaker approached, she was able to use her right hand to force Bui's head into the water so he could get underneath the main force of the wave. She pulled him up once the wave had passed and continued on, swimming for both of them.

She had to continue her struggle to propel them both through the water, and repeat the push and pull action another five or six times until they were around three hundred meters from shore. This far out, the waves had dissipated enough that they no longer had the force to push them back, only causing them to bob about in the swell. Suk Hing felt they were far enough out to take the time to stop and deal with her own ball bladders. She also figured that Bui would be safe enough now. She let go of him to prepare her own floats. As she struggled to get enough air into her lungs to recover from another bout of light-headedness, she looked towards Bui.

He was flopping about slowly in the water, making a feeble attempt to swim. He looked like a dying fish, half-dead already. For the first time, Suk Hing had to admit to herself fully that she didn't think he was going to make it. She could hardly fathom this attitude from her friend. During their brief, clandestine conversations in the prison, Bui had been as determined as she had been, brave and resolute. He had managed to get the note to her, and risked himself by picking her up at the ferry terminal and hiding her in his house. He had trekked for miles, surviving on no food and little water in freezing temperatures. He'd even scaled mountains. How could he possibly give up now? He had been in the same prison with her; he had seen the sheer numbers of people who were captured before they got as far as the third border, never mind the water. He must also have heard the same whispers of those who died in the attempt, having been shot, or starving, or dying of exposure in their emaciated state, or falling to their deaths on the mountains. The landscape itself was home to snakes, wild dogs, and wild boars. Every moment they had spent up there was a risk, yet they had encountered none of those things. None of them had been injured and unable to continue, none of them had died, as far as she knew. She couldn't say for sure as she had no idea how Lum Jong had fared since his mysterious disappearance. She could only hope that since they hadn't found him, neither had the patrols.

Against all odds, she and Bui were in the water, having passed three border controls, almost at a safe distance from shore. He should be ecstatic, overjoyed, filled with a new determination and relief that his new life was within his grasp. Yet here he was, practically comatose beside her, seemingly numb to the possibility of his own freedom.

She hadn't expected this, wasn't prepared for it and didn't understand it. However, she had been forced into this disastrous situation and she had to find a way to deal with it. She wasn't ready to give up on him yet, even if he had given up already. She would just need to be strong enough for both of them. She put the ugly rubber orbs into her net bag and swam over to Bui.

"This is for safety reasons," she told him as she tied her floats around him, giving him extra buoyancy and the best fighting chance of staying above the waterline. "I don't want to have to go back and pick you up again. You can't let me do all this on my own either. I'll do everything I can, but you have to work with me."

Suk Hing removed her pack from her shoulders again and hunted for the twenty-five foot rope. The rope was sodden and heavy, but she managed to tie it around her chest with the knot just above her breastbone. She fished the other end out of the water and wrapped it around Bui, weaving it in and out of the netting then making a knot on his back.

"Right then, enough of this nonsense. You're safe, so pull yourself together. Help me out and swim with me."

Bui still didn't answer, but he made an attempt to follow her lead.

Chapter Seventeen

"The Longer the night, the more dreams there will be"

September 4th, 1966: 11 PM

With Suk Hing doing most of the work, there wasn't much point in trying to fight the tide. They had to swim with it, and as far as she could tell, it was taking them in the direction of Macao.

Suk Hing knew, and wondered if Bui did too, that the waters all around were shark- and barracuda-infested, and probably held an array of other harmful or deadly sea creatures. She also knew that gunboats patrolled the seas and bays, searching for swimmers. During the day, they would be at risk of being spotted by air patrols, which could then easily direct the gunboats to them. She could only hope that between the strong, shifting currents and their own efforts, they would find their way by morning.

Despite all this, the water was actually the safest place for them to be. The gunboats used large searchlights, but the light would reflect off of the water, giving them some natural cover.

She and Bui also had the advantage of being able to hear and see the patrols long before they would be spotted in the vast expanse of water, at least at night. She couldn't say the same for the sharks. She knew they moved swiftly and silently in the water, and would be within striking range before their shadowy fins became visible. Nevertheless, Suk Hing would rather succumb to the depths than give the soldiers the satisfaction of capturing her a second time.

As they swam on, Suk Hing's mind drifted back to her previous attempt. She had learned then that the tide lasted for twelve-hours, but she was struggling to find a way for that information to help her now. She had no idea what time they had entered the water, or what time the tide was due to turn. Hai had known, but he wasn't here. She thought about her two previous companions and wondered what had become of Hai and Kang. She wished there was a way to find out, but there wasn't. She hoped that they had managed to hide long enough for the soldiers to assume they had fled, and then made it to the water, but chances were slim. Being male, they might not have been treated as mildly as she was if they had been captured. She had heard that in other areas, public beatings were frequent, and not just by the soldiers or government officials. Such violence was often carried out by their peers, keen to prove their loyalty to Chairman Mao beyond merely shunning the so-called traitors and turning them and their families into ghosts.

They swam on. Suk Hing thought over everything she had learned during her secret meetings with the group of people who had all been determined to escape. In many ways, she had been lucky in her small town. The propaganda meetings she had to attend were nothing compared to the political rallies that were held in larger places, with the reports of the failed escapees being dragged out and viciously beaten in front of crowds as a warning to others. Had that been the fate of her friends?

Deciding that her thoughts were becoming too dark and morbid, she pulled herself back to the present. Bui was still moving beside her, putting in some effort at least. She couldn't see the moon, but the night sky was filled with stars, and the surface of the water shimmered. It would have been beautiful.

She would have liked to move faster, but had to consider Bui's limitations. She hoped that their movements would be enough to keep some warmth in their muscles as the hours in the cold water bit through to the very marrow in their bones. Cramps and hypothermia were just two of the seemingly countless risks they faced that night, and far from the worst.

There was nothing to see as they swam, only the black, pulsating expanse surrounding them. With Bui in his uncommunicative state, Suk Hing felt just as lonely as she had during her first attempt. She wished he would pull himself together and return to the funny and brave man she knew and cared for deeply.

She estimated that they had been in the water for approximately six hours and had maybe reached the half-way mark when her eyes detected a slight change in the horizon before her. A hazy glow penetrated the blackness in the distance. She couldn't pinpoint anything exact, or focus on it fully, but it thrilled her. She knew it wasn't mainland China, which was mostly pitch-black at night, the only lights being those from the insides of houses. The closest thing she could compare it to was the glow from a distant fire. She was contemplating this when Bui broke his silence.

"Suk Hing, can we stop a minute? I have a pain under my arm."

"I don't think we should stop, Bui. Can you carry on?"

"I'm not sure, it really, really hurts."

"Okay, I'll try to have a look."

Suk Hing trod water alongside Bui, raising his arm and trying to peer at his armpit in the starlight. She sucked in her breath as she saw that the pull of the floats had caused the net to chafe his skin. It had obviously been happening for some time, as the skin had been rubbed raw. It was an angry red, inflamed and bleeding, the net cutting into the groove it had made for itself. It was no wonder Bui was hurting, the wound was open and constantly being doused in salt water. The pain must have been excruciating.

She closed her eyes for a second, trying not to panic. She might be from the country, but everyone knew that blood in the water was the quickest way to attract sharks; they could detect a tiny drop from three miles away. She breathed slowly and deeply through her nose, keeping her fear in check. Her voice was calm when she spoke to Bui.

"I'm afraid you don't have a lot of choice but to carry on. It's the net, Bui, it has chafed your skin a bit and it's obviously hurting in the salt water, that's all. If you were a good enough swimmer, I would remove the floats but you know that we can't. I'll adjust it for you as best as I can, then we have to get moving, we need to get out of this water as quickly as we can."

Bui nodded, miserable, but finally showing a spark of courage as he continued to move through the water. Suk Hing told herself it was pointless, but she couldn't help scanning the immediate area for fins as she swam on. She knew that if she spotted one, there would be nothing she could do, it would be all over, but the logic couldn't prevent her from constantly looking. They swam on for another hour at least, Bui's movement seriously hampered by the level of pain he was experiencing. When he could barely move through the water for himself, Suk Hing had to assist him as she had earlier, swimming for the both of them.

They swam on. The once dim haze was getting brighter and Suk Hing realized that the light had to be coming from streetlights. She had never seen that many lights together in one place. She had never seen anything so bright. It was both frightening and astonishing at the same time. It spurred her on, and she dug deep into her flagging resources to move them more quickly towards the shining beacons in the night.

She slowed her pace, then stopped to tread water. They were closing in on something that spoke of habitation and the hope of dry land in the not-too-distant future. Before them was a large bay, loosely formed by a rough semi-circle of rocks and stones. Suk Hing wasn't certain, but she thought it was a man-made harbour, a place where boats could shelter from typhoons if they had been caught out too far from shore when they hit. If so, it meant that they were still some way from Macau, but it seemed like a perfect place to rest. Suk Hing swam towards it. There were no boats, and no sign of life. Cautiously, she swam them closer, keeping an eye out for any activity that she might have missed in the dark. Save for the insistent hush of the surf, the night was silent. Suk Hing felt certain that the area would provide cover for a short while.

Reaching the rocks, they dragged their exhausted bodies out of the water and over the sharp, jutting stones, until they found a flattish space where they both collapsed. They lay there for almost an hour, trying to regain some strength and enjoy the relief of being safe from the constant threat of drowning or being attacked in the water. Suk Hing was resting, but alert, watching for the sweeping motion of searchlights and listening for the sounds of approaching boats. Suk Hing knew it wasn't over yet. She thought the tide was carrying them in the direction of Macau but she couldn't be certain yet that this was where they had landed. If not, then they were far from safe.

The group from which Suk Hing had received her careful instruction the first time had maintained covert contact with the ones who had made it to Hong Kong. They had informed the leaders of the groups that many people made a serious error at this point. Unable to keep their exact bearings in the water, especially at night, many mistakenly believed they had landed in the safe zone of Macau.

Like Hong Kong, Macau was a special administrative region of China, though it was controlled by the Portuguese. Portugal held sovereignty over the area and it was policed and governed by the Portuguese, not the Chinese. The nearby islands, however, belonged to China and were firmly under communist rule. Many escapees had reached such islands, believing that they were in Macau, safe from the grasp of their hated and feared government, and moved around freely once they reached land, only to be quickly apprehended by the People's Army.

Suk Hing knew she had to try to determine their exact location. If the land she could see in the distance was actually a Chinese island, they would need to get straight back into the water and try to swim in another direction. After untying the rope that joined them and leaving Bui to rest, Suk Hing stood up and stepped carefully to the best vantage point she could find. The land was still a long way off, but as her eyes adjusted to the light after the endless dark, she could see in the far distance the illuminations of what appeared to be not just streetlights, but moving traffic. There were no other visible islands between this bay where she stood and the shore. She began to feel her heart lift with hope. China didn't have such a thing as street lamps; it was dark all through the night. She couldn't absolutely guarantee it, but she was fairly certain she was looking at Macau. They had nearly made it! Delighted, she made her way back to Bui.

She told him what she had seen. Although Bui didn't say much, he looked excited. Suk Hing thought that perhaps he was worried about the final part of the swim. She also hadn't forgotten that he was still in pain from his injury and getting back into the water was the last thing he would want to do. The pressure on the wound had been relieved a little now that the bladders weren't floating and pulling, but it would be just as bad again once they returned to the water. She wished there was more she could do for him, but she could think of nothing. There was still quite a way to swim and the way would become difficult again as they got closer to land, since they would again be vulnerable to the push and pull of the waves washing on the shore.

Once they felt they were ready and had regained enough strength, they slipped off the rocks and sank back into the water. Bui didn't complain. Suk Hing hoped he knew that his suffering would be worth it in the end, if they could only complete this journey.

The absence of boats in the vicinity meant they had a clear line of sight to the shore and a straight swim from their makeshift resting place. It took them approximately twenty minutes to reach the point where they could touch the ground. The sea was relatively calm, meaning they weren't dragged too far back with the ebb and flow and they made good time moving forward. The ground they stepped onto appeared to be an unpleasant mix of sand, mud and dirt. To anyone else, it might have been decidedly unappealing, but to Suk Hing, it was a beautiful sight. As they walked up the beach further onto land, they saw a large, open entryway. They approached it tentatively, their hearts beating wildly and their breathing escaping in ragged bursts. The closer they got, the more details they could make out. They crossed a road to the opening, which appeared to be the entrance to a large vegetable farm. The hour was early, and there were no signs of life, save for a small hut in the middle of a field that had a dim light shining from it.

Thinking the hut had to belong to some form of caretaker or night watchman, Suk Hing felt they should approach, but Bui wasn't convinced.

"What if we aren't where we think we are?"

"We have to be, look at all the lights in the distance."

"I'm not sure, Suk Hing. We've barely been on land for fifteen minutes, should we take risks so soon?"

"I think we have to. Wouldn't it be better to know for sure where we are and get it over with, instead of sneaking around in the dark even longer? Didn't you say you had relatives who lived in Macau?"

"Yes I do, and I have their address memorized."

"Then all we do is ask for directions, we don't need to say anything else."

Bui snorted. "As if we don't look suspicious!"

"Well, true," Suk Hing grinned sheepishly, taking in their sodden and disheveled appearance. "But I still think it's better to know once and for all. Shall we?"

Bui reluctantly agreed and they headed for the small hut and the tiny beacon of light it offered up to them. It took them around twenty minutes to cross the field and Suk Hing kept quiet and kept her pace brisk. She didn't want to give Bui the chance to change his mind. She remembered all too well the fear that had crippled him on several points on their epic journey; she didn't want that to happen again. When she reached the hut, she didn't hesitate or pause for breath, she went right up to the door and gently knocked.

Chapter Eighteen

"When entering a village, follow its customs"

September 5th, 1966: 5 AM

A man appeared instantly at the door. There was a dim light coming from somewhere within, which left the man mostly in silhouette, but Suk Hing could make out that he was an older man, very small and skinny.

He looked them over and asked in low, gentle voice if they'd come from the water. Suk Hing hesitated, assessing the situation. The man appeared to be alone and the farm itself isolated. He was slight, possibly slighter than Suk Hing herself. There was also something reassuring in his voice. After all that had happened, Suk Hing's ears had become well tuned to recognize the tones of deception. She wasn't hearing them now.

Taking a deep breath, she replied,

"Yes, we did."

The man nodded.

"Every night it is the same. People arrive all the time from the water."

"May we trouble you for some directions? My friend has relatives in Macau and we hope to look them up."

The man began shaking his head even before Bui had a chance to tell him the address. "I wouldn't if I were you. You'd be far better off heading into the city and finding the police station. If you report there and tell them of your circumstances, they will get you set up. They will give you a contact name and directions to a nearby refugee camp. From there, you can establish yourselves and get used to things here. That's the best advice I can give."

They thanked the old man and took their leave. As they walked back across the field to the road, Suk Hing and Bui couldn't help smiling. Now there was no doubt that they were in Macau, and, for the moment, safe. Hong Kong would have been best, and life might not be altogether comfortable in a refugee camp, but it would be far better than they had been used to. At the very least, they didn't have to spend every waking minute fearing for their lives.

Certain now that they wouldn't have to flee back into the water, Suk Hing removed the net with the ball bladders from Bui. She put them over her own shoulder, more than happy to carry the small burden. Her body was exhausted and she couldn't remember the last time she had slept, but she felt exhilarated and her mind was in a whirl as they followed the road towards the city.

A reddening in the east signalled dawn, and Bui fumbled about his things to recover his grandfather's watch. Suk Hing was about to ask him for the time, but checked herself. It was clear from the sorrowful look that crossed Bui's face that the watch was no longer working. Suk Hing could have told him that a pocket watch wouldn't have survived the swim unscathed before they entered the water, but there was no point. If she had known before they departed that he had it in his possession, she would have advised him not to take it. Maybe they could have even found some way to waterproof it before the swim. She felt sorry for Bui. The watch was not only beautiful in its own right, it was also an heirloom. It was just another sacrifice that had been made in their quest for a new life. She heard Bui sigh.

"I guess I didn't really expect anything else, but I had some small hope that it would somehow survive."

He raised his arm to throw it away.

"Stop!"

Bui looked at Suk Hing with surprise but lowered his arm. "Why?"

"It's still a family heirloom, and it's still pretty. Perhaps you could have it repaired one day."

Bui shook his head. "No, the casing and insides will rust now that it has been in salt water for so long. We won't be able to save it. Besides, I don't want it. This has been a horrible time and it would only serve as a reminder of it. This is a new start, a new life. Now that I think about it, I don't want anything from the old one."

"If you're absolutely sure you don't want it, may I have it?"

"Why do you want a broken watch?"

"I don't know, but I'd like to keep it if you don't mind."

"I don't mind. Here, if you want it, you have it."

Bui held out the watch and Suk Hing took it, turning it over in her palm.

"Thank you, Bui."

He shrugged. "You're welcome."

She examined the pocket watch, feeling its compact weight in her hand. The silver casing was engraved all over in a tiny pattern front and back, but the focus was an intricate design in the centre. She traced the outline with her fingertip, admiring the detail and craftsmanship that had gone into it. She flipped the watch open to reveal its bold white face encircled with roman numerals. Another smaller dial was inlaid at the bottom of the face, which would have turned to mark the passing seconds. The wheel was still new, and even when it was working, the watch was nearly silent. There was a stamp of some sort on the inside cover, and a maker's name on the face, but Suk Hing could read neither in the half light. Carefully closing the watch, she tucked it away safely into her backpack and turned her mind back to matters at hand.

They both estimated that it was around five a.m., though there was no way to tell for certain. They walked on. It felt strange to be walking on a road, in plain sight, as daylight swelled around them. Out of necessity, they had spent entire days avoiding the sun, like wounded animals desperately camouflaging themselves from the discernment of some relentless predator.

The approaching dawn had already set Suk Hing's nerves on edge when she heard the sound of a vehicle approaching behind them. Suk Hing tensed, but fought the urge to run. Flight had become second nature to her now, and it was a struggle for logic to overcome instinct. Although she kept her eyes straight and carried on waking, she couldn't entirely suppress the panic rising within her as the vehicle passed, stopped a few hundred feet ahead, and U-turned back in their direction. As it approached, Suk Hing could now make out the letters "AICÌLOP" stencilled across the front of a blue jeep. She wasn't quite sure what the word meant, until the jeep came close enough for her to see that it was being driven by two men wearing powder-blue uniforms. Suk Hing and Bui looked anxiously at one another. It had to be the police.

Suk Hing told herself that there was no cause for alarm — they were heading for the police station after all — but she couldn't help but shuffle and swallow nervously as the jeep pulled to a halt alongside them and the officers stepped out. The officers, both perhaps in their mid-thirties, wore friendly expressions as they approached.

"Have you just come from the water, made the swim?"

"Yes, we have," Suk Hing replied for both of them.

"Come on, then. We'll give you a ride to the station. We were heading back there anyway and it's still a very long walk. You must be pretty tired."

Suk Hing could hardly believe her ears. The people here were so friendly and helpful, welcoming even. She hadn't known what to expect, but she hadn't expected this. It was a far cry from the constant victimization and ostracism of her past life. She had only ever known authority as something to be feared and avoided. Here, to Suk Hing's astonishment, the police were actively helping them. For the first time, the pair allowed themselves to relax and become really excited about what the future might hold. Bui was looking all around him like an excited dog, switching from window to window to take in everything they could as they rode in the back of the jeep.

A city gradually appeared, growing out of the horizon like some gargantuan, mythological forest treed in steel and light. Suk Hing gasped at the sheer immensity and beauty of it. Hundreds of streetlights lit up the still dark early morning sky, vehicles with lights on top of them drove around on the roads. The place was filled with wondrous marvels, everything looking so modern and advanced.

"Excuse me," she asked tentatively. "Can you tell me why those vehicles have lights on top of them?"

The officer in the passenger seat turned to look at her. He smiled at her question. "The lights are to show they are taxis. They drive around and you can flag them down and pay them to take you wherever you want to go."

"Taxis," Suk Hing repeated, trying out the unfamiliar word and deciding she liked it. The officer grinned again and Suk Hing blushed, realizing how naive she must have sounded.

The officer driving asked if the two of them were hungry. They admitted they were both ravenous, having eaten the last of the fried flour balls they had with them shortly after scaling the mountain. The jeep pulled into a busy thoroughfare and stopped next to a street vendor. The two officers got out and walked over to the sidewalk, chatting and laughing with the vendor as he prepared their food. Suk Hing and Bui watched on, amazed. The easy interaction between the police and the vendor, the smiles and generally complaisant manner of the people on the streets seemed as foreign to them as anything else in the city. They had both been children when the communist government took power. Neither could remember a day in their lives during that time when anything had been this relaxed.

The officers returned with two steaming bowls, which filled the jeep with a scent that made Suk Hing's mouth water and sent her stomach howling. The two of them had been running on adrenaline for so long that they'd entirely ignored the hunger pangs they had suffered over the last few days. Now they gave in to them completely. The bowls were filled with wonton and noodles in broth, though Suk Hing was so hungry, she would have eaten just about anything put in front of her.

Suk Hing didn't have the words to describe how that meal, eagerly devoured in the back of a police jeep, tasted to her. It was the most wonderful meal she had ever eaten in her life. The last time she had experienced anything close to this was when she was a child living in her family's large estate, before the government had taken everything from them and her father had disappeared, more than sixteen years ago.

As she emptied the bowl, she realized she had been so preoccupied with eating that she hadn't taken the time to thank the two police officers properly. She and Bui made up for it now and told them how grateful they were for their kindness. Suk Hing might have cried at the consideration she was being shown, but she was too thrilled for tears. In China, she was labelled a criminal, a ghost. In Macao, she was being treated as a person; she may be a poor, starving refugee, but here, she was *someone*.

After they had eaten, the officers drove on to the police station. After parking the jeep, the officers led Suk Hing and Bui to the back of a large courtyard. The courtyard's floor was covered in tidy stonework and was open to the darkening sky. Even at this early hour of the morning, people were milling about. Suk Hing estimated there might be around two hundred of them there. They all looked on the youngish side and fit, if slightly on the skinny side. No one seemed inclined to talk, but Suk Hing surmised that they were all refugees who had made the swim from mainland China. She and Bui followed suit and sat quietly in a corner, and waited.

A nearby clock tower chimed 8 a.m. A small group of people in aprons began moving into the courtyard and serving steamed buns and cups of milk. Suk Hing stared, incredulous. She couldn't remember the last time she had seen such a thing. In her experience, only those with a special note from the doctor received milk. It wasn't something that was accessible to any ordinary person. She and Bui devoured these unexpected treats with relish. They noticed that a line had begun to form at the doors to the office, so they joined the others in the queue.

At 9 a.m., the office doors opened and the first in line were taken inside. The queue was moving slowly so, to amuse herself, Suk Hing began studying the people around her in the courtyard. Scanning a group of refugees forming line on the other side of the enclosure, she was astonished to see a familiar face.

"Lum Jong!" she called out happily.

Startled, Lum Jong turned in the direction of his name. His face broke into a smile as he spotted them and Suk Hing laughed. She was so happy to find out that not only was Lum Jong alive and well, but he was here, safe. She was practically jumping with excitement.

"Let's meet out here afterwards," she cried to him and he nodded. They had to wait a long time until they were granted access to the office, but in her joy Suk Hing found the hours passing with ease. She didn't think she had ever had so much to be thankful for at once in her life.

When Suk Hing and Bui finally reached the office interior, they found themselves standing before three officials in grey uniforms seated at a long table. Suk Hing was prepared to say anything, true or not, to get through. The official seated in the middle smiled, took their names, hastily stamped two documents, handed them to Suk Hing and Bui, and motioned them on their way. Just like that, they were now "officially" refugees.

Lum Jong was already in the courtyard waiting for them and Suk Hing ran to him, greeting him with an ear-to-ear grin.

"I'm so pleased to see you! We looked everywhere for you in every direction but you had completely disappeared. What happened?"

"I just ran and hid like you did. I laid low for as long as possible. When I thought the coast was clear, I searched for you too but couldn't find you. To be honest, I thought that you had been caught. Once I'd come to that conclusion, I just took off, running for the water."

"I told Bui that's exactly what you would do, didn't I?" Suk Hing turned to Bui and gave him a playful nudge.

"You did," Bui admitted, laughing.

They stood together for a while, talking and laughing with each other. Soon, the police escorted them to a large bus. The three of them climbed aboard and were taken to a church high on a hill. As the bus pulled to a halt they were asked to disembark and line up. Everyone was happy to assent; it was more of a pleasant request than an order, and everything that had happened so far had led Suk Hing to believe that they were in safe hands.

Once the line had moved within the church, Suk Hing saw that the refugees were being ferried through a series of stations providing them with a variety of supplies. At the first station, they were given a food card. This wasn't a certificate permitting them to buy food like the one Suk Hing used to require back home. Rather, the food card the refugees were given would allow them to receive free food from certain street vendors in the city. Apparently, anyone and everyone had the right to food here. The way the refugees looked at the card, it could have been made of solid gold. At another station, she was handed a new pair of shoes, two shirts, two pairs of pants, and two pairs of socks. At the final station, Suk Hing was shocked to receive twenty-five Yuan. Considering her yearly wages in China were seventy-five yen, this felt like an absolute fortune to have in her hand at once. She could hardly believe it.

Everything was given freely and without a grudge, and she began to realize that the way people lived in her country was far from normal. This was normal; this was humanity.

When she heard Bui and Lum Jong cheering along with the others at the announcement that they would be able to stay at the refugee camp for up to six weeks, Suk Hing's heart and spirits lifted even further. Not only had she found her lost friend, but her other friend was slowly getting back to his old self, losing the debilitating terror and fear that had been plaguing him since the day they had set off. At that moment, she didn't think life could get any better. She had friends, food, a place to stay, warm, dry clothes to wear, but most of all, she had freedom, and she had hope.

Chapter Nineteen

"Rain past, heaven bright"

September 5th, 1966: 10 AM

Suk Hing wandered outside with her bundles of supplies, overwhelmed by the kindness and generosity shown
to her. She was in a daze, but soon pulled herself back to
her normal, practical way of thinking when she spotted a
telephone. For some time, she'd had the telephone number
of one of her half-brothers in Hong Kong. She had never
before dared to use the number, as contact with any defectors was forbidden, but now she felt it was safe to do so.
With shaking fingers, she dialled the number, hoping her
half-brother Quan was still at the same place.

Suk Hing was relieved when Quan did indeed answer
the telephone. He was delighted that she had made it to

Macau, telling her how brave she had been and how well she had done. After catching up for a few moments, he told her she should look up an old friend of his. His friend owned a bike shop in town called *Dongli Feixin*, which meant "to Power Fly." Quan gave her a name, address, and directions. Suk Hing repeated the information back, ensuring she had it memorized. Once they were certain she had the details correct, her half-brother told her he would take the ferry to Macau within a couple of days and would meet her at his friend's shop. Suk Hing confirmed that she would look forward to seeing him there and they ended the call on a happy note.

Bui and Lum Jong were waiting for her when she finished the call and they informed her they were to find their own way to the camp. They had been given directions from the people in the church. In high spirits, the three of them set off on the half-hour walk to their temporary new home. They recognized the camp instantly as it came into view. There was no mistaking it. It was a large barn-like structure with several people milling about outside. Inside, there was row upon row of bunk beds and little else. The place was intended for sleeping only, providing shelter and a soft bed. It reminded Suk Hing a little of the prison in which she and Bui had first been incarcerated on their capture, but this time there were no guards preventing them from talking and they were free to come and go from the camp as much as they wanted to, and at any time.

After placing their items on a bed, the three of them wandered outside. Suk Hing went to talk to other people, gaining knowledge about the local area. However, it wasn't long before the lack of sleep during the long journey took its toll. The sleep they had managed to snatch here and there during the escape was tense and unsatisfactory, the danger never leaving their minds and causing them to waken at the slightest sound. When Suk Hing crawled into her safe bunk, she slept soundly, despite the number of people around her.

Waking early the next morning, Suk Hing said her goodbyes to Bui and Lum Jong.

"My brother's arriving in a couple of days. We're meeting at a shop in town and from there, I hope, we're heading to Hong Kong."

Lum was ecstatic.

"That's amazing! Hong Kong! We're so happy for you, Suk Hing!"

Lum jostled Bui, who smiled weakly.

"What's wrong, Bui?," Suk Hing asked.

Bui hesitated.

"Nothing. It's nothing. I'm…I'm happy for you Suk Hing. Really."

Bui placed his hands gently on Suk Hing's shoulders.

"The only reason I'm here is because of you. I'd be dead."

"It's all right, Bui. We made it. It doesn't matter how."

Suk Hing removed Bui's grandfather's watch from her pocket and held it in front of her.

"Last chance," Suk Hing smiled.

"You keep it. The watch is broken, but time moves forward. I need to move forward, too."

"Whatever you feel is best, Bui."

"Just remember," Lum joked, "it'll still be right twice a day!"

The three friends embraced a final time. Suk Hing turned and made her way into the city of Macau, whose narrow, angular streets soon obscured Lum and Bui from Suk Hing's view.

Suk Hing turned Bui's grandfather's watch over in her hands and, as she did, also turned over Bui's words in her mind. The watch was, perhaps, literally broken, but Suk Hing had taken from this a different lesson than Bui had. It was, of course, impossible to know for certain when the watch had actually stopped, but Suk Hing imagined that its hands may have rested the moment they had broken free, and were finally safe. Perhaps the watch now marked the very moment that their own histories had broken in two.

Suk Hing made her way to one of the local vendors who accepted her food card and ate a hasty, though satisfying breakfast. The bike shop wasn't supposed to be far — by her half-brother's estimate, it was a twenty or thirty minute walk from the refugee camp — but Suk Hing was eager to find it so that she might begin the next stage of her journey. Recalling Quan's directions, she soon found herself standing before the small shop, which had been squeezed between two larger ones, with the words *Dongli Feixin* painted in swooping, slightly cracked, letters across its window.

Suk Hing opened the door and stepped tentatively inside. Within, she found an older man, perhaps in his fifties. He was of average height and build, and had short grey hair. Suk Hing noticed a hardness to the man, the look of someone who had spent much of his life working.

She approached the man and introduced herself. He spoke little, merely confirming that her brother had contacted him and told him to expect her. He directed her to the rear of the shop. Despite the man's overall reticence, he seemed pleasant enough, and Suk Hing felt confident she could follow him without reservation.

At the back of the shop sat a small woman tending a young child. Suk Hing introduced herself and the woman greeted her pleasantly. The woman eagerly inquired about Suk Hing's escape and she obliged, relating the tale of the freedom swim. Suk Hing couldn't help but notice that while the mother looked healthy, even a little plump compared to the emaciated people she remembered from her hometown, the child looked pale and sickly. Once she had satisfied the woman's curiosity about her trip, Suk Hing turned the conversation to the child.

"How old is your little boy?"

"He's just turned one year old, but you wouldn't think it would you? He's too small for his age, and he's not in the best health."

"I'm sorry to hear that. What's the matter with him?"

The mother went on to explain that the child was suffering from a complicated blood disorder. Unfortunately, neither she nor her husband's blood types were compatible, and finding a donor had been difficult.

"What type of blood do you have?" the woman suddenly asked.

"To be honest, I have no idea. Is there a way to find out?"

"Yes, the hospital can do a very quick and easy test."

"Good," Suk Hing nodded. "Then we can go to the hospital and we can find out if my blood could be of any use."

The woman smiled gratefully at Suk Hing. "Thank you so much, we can go tomorrow morning. For now, I'd better start preparing dinner."

Surprised at the amount of time that had passed while they had been talking, Suk Hing offered to help and the two women made dinner together. She sat and ate with the family, enjoying every mouthful.

After dinner was finished and cleared away, the shopkeeper addressed Suk Hing:

"I'm afraid we have no room upstairs. You're welcome here, but you will have to sleep in the shop. Perhaps you would prefer to go back to the camp where you can sleep on a proper bed?"

"I'd be very grateful if I could sleep here," Suk Hing replied. "Then we could set off early in the morning for the hospital. I don't mind sleeping in the shop. I've slept in far worse places."

The man acknowledged her request with a nod and the woman went to fetch what she could for Suk Hing to set up a makeshift bed. However sparse the accommodation, the floor of a bicycle shop was still infinitely more comfortable than the mountainside burrow, or the grave-like pit in which she spent nights during the escape. She lay down beneath the suspended bicycle frames as the last of the daylight streamed through the shop's dusty windows, throwing a manifold of spoke shadows across the shop walls. Suk Hing thought of the sunlight dappling through her grandmother's lychee trees. She thought about the different ways people encountered one another in different circumstances. In China, people rarely helped one another. Yes, she had met some good people, people who were kind and trustworthy, but she felt they were the exception and not the rule. The communist regime had turned most people into something they probably thought they could never be. Many to her seemed heartless, selfish, turning on one another simply to curry favour with the soldiers for a short time, willing to do anything for some extra food or less brutal treatment. Suk Hing was shocked that a government could change so many people for the worse, but she had seen it with her own eyes. Here, the goodness inside of people was still on the outside, too; people still had understanding and compassion. They still had problems — she thought of the child with bad blood lying above her — but were willing to put themselves out for others, to share what they had, however little. She thought of the child again and wondered if her blood would match, allowing her to help and repay the family's kindness. Drifting closer to sleep, the image of the child before her shifted and in the twilight looked a little less pale.

The next morning, Suk Hing and her hostess made the trip to the hospital. Suk Hing took a seat and her thumb was pricked. She smeared the tiny drop of blood onto a card, which a nurse then collected and hurried away. When the nurse returned, she was smiling: Suk Hing's blood was compatible. The nurses took her to a room where her arm was wiped with alcohol and a needle inserted. The nurse carefully filled several tubes of her blood and labelled them. Once they had taken what they needed, Suk Hing stood to leave. She felt a little light-headed, but otherwise fine. By the time she had made the walk back to the shop, she was back to normal.

The family were very grateful, but Suk Hing insisted it was the least she could do after the kindness they had shown her. She sat with the mother and the baby in the back room, passing the time chatting and gently playing with the sickly child. Suk Hing hoped her blood would make a difference.

It was around one p.m. when Suk Hing's half-brother Quan arrived at the shop. Suk Hing peeked at him from the back of the store. Quan appeared to be in his mid-thirties and seemed taller and thinner than she remembered. He spoke to the storeowner for a long time, and Suk Hing got the impression that her brother really liked to talk. Finally, he came through to the back and greeted his long lost half-sister.

"There you are, Suk Hing! Have you been eavesdropping on us this whole time? I didn't even see you there. With stealth like that, it's no wonder you escaped! I never thought, in a million years, that I'd be seeing you here. Not in a million years! But here you are! Grown up, too. Well, I don't suppose you wouldn't have grown at all, it *has* been years, hasn't it? I've grown too, mostly around the waist! Ha!…"

At various points Suk Hing attempted to respond to her half-brother's queries, but it wasn't apparent that he had any intention of pausing long enough to allow it. In the interest of leaving the shop sometime in the next month, Suk Hing decided to politely interrupt him to say goodbye and thank you to the shop owners. When they finally left the store and eased their way into the streets, it was Suk Hing's turn to speak. She plied her brother with question after question, about Hong Kong, when they might possibly depart, how they would get there, and what she might do when they arrived. Her brother listened, smiling, gently guiding her through the narrow streets and the lively afternoon foot-traffic.

"We cannot go to Hong Kong now, Suk Hing, at least not yet. First, you need to get back on your feet. By that I mean you'll need some money. It is difficult to find work anywhere, even here, and especially in Hong Kong. It's even more difficult to get by without any money of your own. You can't be a refugee forever. Sooner or later, the state's charity dries up. But, I have friends here who can give you work. When you save up enough, and are better adjusted to life here, I can take you to Hong Kong."

Suk Hing soon realized that Quan's occasional gesturing this way or that were wholly intentional. She had been so preoccupied with the idea of getting to Hong Kong that she had barely noticed that her half-brother had led her to the cast-iron gates of what appeared to be a large factory. They went in and were quickly approached by a tall, handsome man who looked to be close to her half-brother's age. Quan and the man greeted each other warmly, like old friends, and began talking. Suk Hing stood by half-listening and half-surveying the factory floor, which was lined with row upon row of long tables, each humming with the rhythm of dozens of industrial sewing machines. There were few, if any, women using the machines themselves. Most were moving about and between the machines, examining bolts of cloth and placing them into wide rectangular bins. A variety of irregular textiles hung limply over a bin marked with the Portuguese word, *Refugo*. Finally, the handsome man approached her and introduced himself as the owner of the factory.

"Your brother tells me that you are a very hard worker and that you're looking for a job, is that right?"

"Yes," Suk Hing replied. "I'm a fast learner so I'm sure I could pick up any job quickly."

"So you would be happy with factory work?"

"Of course," she replied, recalling her half-brother's remark that jobs weren't easy to come by, even in Macau. She couldn't afford to be choosy, and if Quan had contacts, she ought to take advantage of them, regardless of the work. In any case, she was grateful for the chance to work and earn some money of her own. She was also certain that working in the factory couldn't be as bad as toiling in the fields of the state-run farms back home.

"Okay then, there is a position in quality assurance. We have knitting machines, but each garment has to be carefully checked for errors or flaws after the machine is finished. Do you think you can handle that?"

"Absolutely," Suk Hing replied enthusiastically.

The man laughed. "Good to hear you're so keen, but the shifts are long and tiring. You would be working for fourteen hours a day, seven days a week. Still think you can handle it?"

"I'm sure of it," she replied confidently. She had worked longer hours in a much more physical job. She didn't doubt her own determination to succeed.

"Then the job's yours. The wages are one hundred and seventy five *escudo* per month. What about accommodation, do you have a place to stay?"

Suk Hing struggled to answer the question; she still hadn't wrapped her mind around what, to her ears, sounded like an astronomical sum of money. One hundred and seventy five *escudo* seemed like an absolute fortune. She couldn't believe her luck. His expectant face reminded her that he was waiting for an answer.

"A place to stay? Umm, well, no, not really. I have a bed at the camp for a few weeks."

The factory owner nodded understandingly. "My cousin rents out a couple of rooms. It just so happens that there is a room available. Would you like me to set that up for you?"

Suk Hing didn't care what the room was like; she would have a place of her own, paid for with her own earnings. There was no hesitation in answering. "That would be wonderful, thank you!"

"Great, let's get all the details settled."

Suk Hing followed him to the office where everything was organized. As she left with her new address on a piece of paper and her instructions to arrive at the factory the next morning, it finally dawned on her that she was about to begin her new life, one free of the horrors of communism.

Chapter Twenty

"The ship will reach the end of the bridge in due course"

November 1966

For the next two months Suk Hing woke up at 5 a.m., ate breakfast, worked for fourteen hours, ate dinner, then slept again. Her room, located at the very top of the factory owner's cousin's building, was dingy and cramped. It didn't really matter what it was like, she spent so little time there. Despite how high her wages had sounded initially, the higher quality of life in Macau meant that even sundry items were expensive. The factory owner's cousin charged fifty *escudo* per month in rent, but after food and other expenses, there was very little left of Suk Hing's monthly wages. Suk Hing had prided herself on having been able to do much with little after the Chinese government displaced her once wealthy family, but no matter how frugal she was on her own while in Macau, she was struggling just to get by.

The factory work itself was its own kind of struggle, at once monotonous and requiring a painstaking attention to detail. And yet, Suk Hing remained incredibly grateful. She needed only remind herself of her prior working conditions: the mud-bound, parasite-ridden fields, the inhospitable rice and sugar plants, the vicious young soldiers. Life in Macau had taken on a kind of monochrome haze, to be sure, but it was a benign haze, like the white noise of the sewing machines in the factory itself, which after a few hours seemed to envelop everything, but whose thrum reminded Suk Hing that she was somewhere warm and dry and civilized.

Suk Hing tried to keep in touch with Bui and Lum Jong, but the long working hours made it hard. She learned that they both had found jobs and accommodations of their own, and she was happy that they too were making lives for themselves. Lum Jong had taken a job as a bicycle courier, which suited him. Bui never said much about where he was working. Suk Hing suspected that the relatives he had in Macau were wealthy and were more or less supporting him. It wasn't her business so she didn't ask questions. They usually managed to meet up once every two or three weeks, taking walks together in a park area close to Suk Hing's apartment. Those times spent with her friends were the highlights of her current life.

The first two months passed quickly. Suk Hing was generally content with how things were going, but soon, things began to change. Tensions were rising both in the factory and in the streets. Suk Hing wasn't entirely sure what was going on, but she couldn't ignore the growing sense of unease around her. She made a point of listening to conversations in the factory and on the street as she walked to and from work. She couldn't be entirely certain, but overheard enough to know that it was to do with the Chinese government. It sounded as though communists and communist sympathizers were meddling in the affairs of the Portuguese-run city. Suk Hing didn't want to involve herself in any discussions regarding the matter so didn't ask any questions, but her fear and hatred of the government and what it had done to her country and people left her as anxious about the situation as the others around her.

She worked on, and kept mostly to herself until finally, on December 3, 1966, things came to breaking point. Thousands of people gathered to protest in the streets, chanting slogans and making demands from the Portuguese government. She later discovered that the protests had been triggered by a clash between the police and a group of Chinese who, a couple of weeks earlier, had attempted to build a school without the proper building permits. The school had been financially backed by an organization with leftist sympathies, and who had in turn refused to deal with what they believed were deeply corrupt Portuguese city officials. Fighting ensued. Forty Chinese were injured in the conflict, and over a dozen arrested. Now the Chinese population were demanding a public apology and repara-tion for the injured parties, as well as a promise that force would never be used against them again.

The crowd's outrage intensified until the protest devolved into a full-scale riot. The factory workers were sent home. Suk Hing raced through the frenetic streets, seeking shelter back in her room. Though moving as quickly as possible through the crowds, Suk Hing picked up snatches of phrases amidst the rising cacophony that sounded eerily familiar:

"… martyrs have heroically laid down their lives for the people; let us hold their banner high and march ahead…"

"… fear no sacrifice and surmount every difficulty to win victory…"

"… we must unite with the proletariat of all the capitalist countries…"

"…the whole world will belong to the people…"

Then she noticed something else. Many of the protesters were carrying books, small books with bright red covers, embossed with the Chinese golden star. She hurried on.

From her room's window high above the streets, she watched aghast as the riot unfolded itself across the city. Mobs thronged the attenuated straits and alleys like angry blood thickening to seize the city's heart. Somewhere gunshots rang out. Small pyres, fuelled by books without red covers, dotted the streets and plazas. Suk Hing could no longer see the large statue of the Portuguese Colonel that marked the centre of the city.

The violence lasted well into the next morning. Suk Hing spent the rest of the night listening to news updates on her small radio. The Portuguese government had declared martial law. Everything was shut down, including the textile factories. The people were under curfew from nine p.m. to six a.m., but with the factory closed, there wasn't anywhere for Suk Hing to go anyway. She lay on her bed, listening anxiously as swells of shouting, police sirens, gunfire, and even the occasional explosion echoed around her. Suk Hing wondered why this had to happen now, just when she had thought she was free from the terrors of communism, just as she was settling into her new life. The city, and her new life, was coming apart.

A few days later, Suk Hing managed to contact Quan. As long as the city was under martial law, the factories remained closed, and it was unclear when, or whether, they would reopen. Quan was still the only person she knew who had the contacts that would allow her to find new work, which she needed, and quickly, or she would risk losing her room. He didn't let her down. Less than 48 hours later, he found her a position as a housekeeper to a retired doctor who was in ill health.

For the two weeks that the riots continued, Suk Hing worked there, tending to the house, the doctor, and his family. The doctor himself was a nice man, grateful for her assistance and pleasant to work for, but his wife was different. She was very particular and fussy, finding fault with the way Suk Hing did things and constantly berating her. It was a trying time for Suk Hing, with the nagging doctor's wife, sleepless nights, the constant threat of violence when making her way to and from work, and the uncertainty about the outcome of the riots. She tried to avoid the conflict whenever she could, using alternative routes to stay away from the worst of the fighting.

Although the political situation was far from resolved, the rioting and protesting began to calm down after a couple of weeks. The city began to return to normal; the curfew was lifted and the factories were allowed to open once again. Suk Hing was able to return to her previous job and for the next three months her life resumed its mundane pattern of getting up, working, eating, sleeping and rising the next morning to do it all over again. She was disappointed that she wasn't able to save more money. She was desperate to start sending money back home, but it was always just beyond her means. She also constantly worried about the political situation in Macau. Things were quiet for now but she had no idea how long that would last. It seemed as if she could never outrun the grasp of communism.

One day, Quan turned up on her doorstep and handed her an envelope. Before she had a chance to open it, he told her to start packing her things; it was time for her to go. She nervously opened the envelope and examined the contents: a boarding pass and immigration papers that would allow her to enter Hong Kong. Looking more closely at the paperwork, she was surprised to see someone else's name written beneath her photograph. She knew better than to ask Quan for particulars. She would be whoever she needed to be if it meant getting into Hong Kong.

That morning, Suk Hing went to work as normal, but instead of quietly departing at the end of her fourteen-hour shift as usual, she made her way across the floor to the factory owner's office, and informed him that she was quitting. She spent the next day packing and tying up loose ends, giving up the lease on her room and settling any bills she owed. She wanted to say goodbye to her friends, but decided that the fewer people that knew of her leaving, the better. She tried to keep a low profile, giving her former boss and landlord evasive answers when they asked where she was moving to. Soon, it was departure day.

As previously arranged, she and her half-brother arrived at the dock separately and queued in separate lines, pretending they were strangers. If the forged paperwork failed to fool the authorities, Suk Hing did not want her brother implicated in the subterfuge. Though the forged documents hadn't been strictly necessary, both Suk Hing and Quan agreed that covering their tracks as much as possible was best. The protests had eventually led the Portuguese Governor to tender an official apology to the Macanese Chinese population, an apology which he issued while standing under a portrait of Chairman Mao. Rumours swirled that Portugal's control over Macau had effectively come to an end. Since Suk Hing, along with various members of her family, were still "persons of interest" where the Chinese government was concerned, it would be safer to cross into Hong Kong as anonymously as possible. Suk Hing had no idea how much her half-brother had paid for the documents, but she guessed the price had been a small fortune at least. He hadn't mentioned the money when he handed over the documents and ticket, and Suk Hing felt it would have been impolite to ask. He had gone to extraordinary lengths to help her since her arrival in Macau, and she felt the very least she could do was keep him out of trouble and suffer the consequences alone if things went wrong.

After all that she had been through, she wasn't too concerned when handing over the false paperwork to the authorities on the dock. She remained completely calm while the paperwork was examined, the guard looking from her face back to the photograph on the documents. With a brief nod, he handed the documents back to her, waving her on. She kept her relief in check as she realized she had been cleared to board the ship. She made her way causally on board. As the boat pulled away from the dock, her brother came to find her. This was it; she was finally on her way to Hong Kong.

Chapter Twenty-One

"One joy scatters a hundred griefs"

February 12ᵗʰ, 1967: 6 AM

The crossing took approximately three hours, though for Suk Hing it felt much longer. It was a monumental sight, watching mainland China retreating in the distance. How long she had been striving for this very outcome, and how much she had endured to get to this point. It felt like it had taken a lifetime. She couldn't wait for the ferry to dock and to finally set foot in what she hoped was the land of freedom and opportunity.

When the moment did arrive, it felt almost anticlimactic. The docks were bustling with people waiting to board and people anxious to disembark. People going about their business. There was no time to savour that first step onto land, no time to add ceremony to the occasion, as Suk Hing hurried to keep up with her brother through the crowds. She barely had time to take in the scenery or get her bearings as he immediately whisked her away from the dockyard, through the streets to his home.

On arrival Suk Hing was greeted by family. All of her brothers who had previously succeeded on the journey were waiting to meet her, including her full brother from whom she had been separated ever since she had left to live with her grandmother. The last she had heard of her brother he had been captured and had been sent to a commune to work after his prison sentence. She was overjoyed to see him there.

"Kin Mou," she exclaimed. "You made it!"

He grinned back at her. "Yes I did, and so have you. Not so small and delicate now, are you?"

"I have you to thank for making it. Those words seem so long ago, but they were the ones that gave me the idea and spurred me on to train at the pool, gathering the strength to make the trip."

"Thinking of you back then I wouldn't have believed you could do it. I should have known better. You were always so determined and stubborn. I'm glad I had a hand in your escape."

"You did more than that, although indirectly. It was because you were my brother that the rebel group finally trusted me and agreed to help, and then Chang Chang set up a safe house for me to use on my first attempt..."

Kin Mou raised his eyebrows. "*First* attempt?"

"I failed that time. I ended up in jail, for a time. It was humiliating, but it was because of that safe house that I met Bui, who I travelled with the second time. And here I am!"

The family spent a few happy hours catching up and sharing stories. One of her half-brothers offered her a job sewing in his factory and she was quick to accept. She would start the very next day.

Suk Hing began yet another new life. She stayed with her brother initially and worked at the factory. As always, the hours were long and work consumed most of her life. Money was still tight, but she able to set up an arrangement with a cousin to send ten dollars a month to her mother back home. She still didn't dare communicate with her directly, but it put her mind at ease a little to know that she was receiving the money. She imagined her mother eating decent meals and not the disgusting soybean and turnip dishes they had survived on before. She even imagined her being able to buy medicine to help her with her pain. She was as content with the arrangement as she could be. She had known it would be hard to leave her, but she could have done nothing for her by remaining in the town.

It didn't take long for the relative peace of her new life to be shattered once again. Rumours started in the factory regarding a pro-communist movement in the area and support for a communist government grew. People began walking around carrying the little red book in their hands. Suk Hing now had the opportunity to inspect it more closely than she had in Macau: it was, as she suspected, a publication of selected statements, speeches and writings by Chairman Mao. She didn't know whether to scream or cry when she heard the declarations of some in the factory:

"Once Mao Zedong's thought is grasped by the masses, it becomes an inexhaustible source of strength and a spiritual atom bomb of infinite power!"

She could have quoted that phrase, and dozens of others, in her sleep. It chilled her blood to hear them again, and to know that people were voluntarily seeking them out, here, where life was fair and they didn't have soldiers forcing them to follow his teachings.

The previous year, in 1966, Chairman Mao had mobilized a mass paramilitary social movement of young people to help bolster the cause of the Cultural Revolution both in China and abroad. For all of the slogans in the little red book denouncing imperial policy, Mao had no problem compromising the independence of other nations to spread his own "revolutionary" brand of imperialism. Now, people in Hong Kong were affiliating themselves with that movement, calling themselves the Red Guard, and causing problems, riling up workers, and fomenting discord amongst the general populace. Suk Hing despised these people who had never lived under the constant despair of the communist rule, had never had their home and belongings ripped from them, had never had their family torn apart or been denied earning and keeping a decent wage. What did they truly know of communist rule? They only heard and believed the idealistic propaganda, instead of living through the beatings, the starvation, and the indignity of mass body collections for the dead. She wished she could tell them the truth of it all, but they wouldn't listen even if she tried. Instead, she kept her feelings hidden and avoided the supporters at all costs.

The entire city was tense, and after her experience in Macau, Suk Hing was afraid that the pro-communist movement would gain further traction, causing major disruptions. In May 1967, protests began at the factory. People were again raising their little red books, chanting communist slogans, and denouncing British colonial rule. Demonstrations broke out all over the city, and over the next few months, things only got worse.

Soon, there was fighting in the streets. Gunfire could be heard all through the night, just like in Macau. Bombs and explosions began to rock the hours of darkness. In Beijing, the Red Guard pillaged and then burnt down the British embassy. Sympathizers mounted speakers on the Bank of China building, which blared pro-communist rhetoric. The city was placed under curfew and other drastic measures were put in place in order to try to quell the demonstrations. Leftist newspapers and schools were shut down. The police began mass raids of suspected leftist strongholds and made hundreds of arrests, while communist sympathizers took over various government-owned buildings, turning much of Hong Kong's major commercial and financial districts into militarized zones. Suk Hing continued to keep her disgust of the communist government a closely held secret. Her only consolation during these troubled times was an update from her cousin that her mother was fine. It wasn't much, but the short communication was enough to boost Suk Hing's flagging spirits.

Eventually, the rioting and the troubles were brought under control. After eighteen months of violence, the Chinese Prime Minister ordered leftist groups in Hong Kong to cease their attacks. Life in Hong Kong slowly returned to normal and Suk Hing went back to work at the factory.

Chapter Twenty-Two

"Love house and crow"

February 1970

Almost three years had passed when Suk Hing's world was once again turned upside down. One February day in 1970, Suk Hing made one of her frequent trips to visit Kin Mou at his apartment. She was friendly or familiar with many of his neighbours that lived in the building. During this particular visit, Suk Hing ran into the middle-aged lady who lived upstairs. She and her brother had known the woman for a while and considered her a close friend. After greeting each other, the woman looked coquettishly at Suk Hing.

"Will you come upstairs and see me before you leave today?"

"Of course," Suk Hing agreed. "There's nothing wrong is there?" Worry crossed Suk Hing's face, but the woman attempted to allay her fears.

"No, not at all, I would just like you to come up before you go."

Relating the conversation to her brother, they both agreed she should go up sooner rather than later. Keen to satisfy her curiosity, Suk Hing headed upstairs and knocked tentatively on the door. The door opened and the woman quickly ushered her inside. Suk Hing was surprised to see a young, slender, handsome man standing, somewhat awkwardly, in the living room.

"Suk Hing, this is my nephew, Gai Kwong."

The woman insisted they both sit down and chat, then bustled off to the kitchen to prepare refreshments. Embarrassed, Suk Hing nervously glanced at Gai. His features were sharp and handsome. He had jet-black hair, which he wore swept back in a way that made him look like some of the American rock 'n rollers Suk Hing had sometimes glanced on the covers of magazines. She soon forgot her nerves as they began talking and getting to know one another. Conversation seemed to flow naturally and easily between them and by the end of the visit Gai Kwong asked for permission to see her again. To the delight of her brother's neighbour, Suk Hing readily agreed and they made arrangements for him to call on her next week. Suk Hing returned to her brother's apartment, aflutter with excitement. Kin Mou, noticing the conspicuous flush on his sister's cheek, asked if anything was wrong. Suk Hing smiled.

"No, not at all."

Suk Hing spent the next week in a blur of nervous anticipation, daydreaming about the moment of her next meeting with Gai while she worked, musing about how things would go. She was surprised to be so affected by one meeting with the young man, but she had felt an instant connection to him that she hadn't experienced in her life before. There was something about him that put her at ease.

As he pulled up outside on a Yamaha motorcycle exactly on time, Suk Hing ran downstairs to meet him. After saying hello, she climbed on the back of the bike and Gai Kwong took her out for dinner. Over the meal, he told her many things about himself. She was fascinated to discover that his family had emigrated from Hong Kong to Canada some years ago and he was only back in Hong Kong to visit remaining family, including his aunt, the upstairs neighbour. He talked enthusiastically about the beauty of Canada, enthralling Suk Hing with the tales of how different it was. He made it sound almost magical: the almost unimaginable size of it, and the snow that blanketed everything for months and which glittered in the winter sun like fallen stars. The evening passed much too quickly and Suk Hing was disappointed when it was time to go. They arranged to meet again the next week at the same time. Suk Hing was on cloud nine as she let herself into her home.

The work week dragged on until it was time to see Gai Kwong again. She spent most of her time thinking about him, and about all the things he had told her of Canada and how different life was there. The smallest details of their conversation would come back to her. When she had admired his hair, he told her he modelled the style on a "very popular singer" named Elvis Presley. Suk Hing had never heard of him, but could only imagine a place where a role model was an entertainer and not a political figure. The sense of freedom that vision suggested was unknown to her, even living in Hong Kong.

Gai stayed in Hong Kong for over a year. Once a week he would take Suk Hing out on a date. Sometimes they went for dinner, other times for coffee. They spent many happy hours strolling in the nearby parks or watching movies in a darkened theatre. He behaved like a perfect gentleman, and even her brothers could find no fault with her suitor. After a year of dating, Suk Hing had to admit to herself that she was in love.

In April 1971, Gai made an unexpected visit to Suk Hing. He took her hand as he explained his reason for turning up unannounced.

"I've had word from my family in Canada. My father has taken ill. He's had a stroke and his condition's serious. I have to return home straight away."

Suk Hing was devastated, both for Gai Kwong and his family, and the fact that he was leaving. Still, she knew that his place was by his father's side right now.

"I understand," she told him.

"Suk Hing, I have something I want to ask you before I go."

"You can ask me anything."

Gai nervously cleared his throat before he spoke. "I love you, Suk Hing. Will you come back to Canada with me and do me the honor of marrying me?"

Suk Hing gasped. Though she had often dreamt of such a proposal, she hadn't expected one so soon. She also hadn't expected to have to make the decision so quickly. Moving to another country and leaving everyone and everything that she knew behind was a huge decision, even though she loved Gai dearly.

"I can't go with you right now. I need time to think it all over. I hope you can understand that, it's just too sudden."

Gai sighed. "I do understand. I'm sorry we have to part like this. Here, I'll give you all my contact information, please keep in touch."

"I will, I promise."

With that, Gai Kwong was gone, heading back to a place called Alberta in Canada.

Suk Hing was bereft. She missed him far more than she believed possible. Her life seemed empty without him, and she was no longer content to spend her days filled with work alone. For all that she had lost in life, losing Gai, however temporarily, hurt the most. In May, a few weeks after Gai Kwong had left, she sat down to attempt to compose a proper letter for the first time in her life.

Suk Hing told her mother everything that had happened to her since she had successfully reached Macau as though she was experiencing it all again herself. Then she began to write the hardest part of the letter. Suk Hing struggled not only with the characters on the page, but with her emotions. Revealing her innermost feelings to her mother was an experience completely foreign to her.

… Even though my heart tells me I must write this letter, my head is telling me how dangerous it is, and how much

harm could come to you because of it. I pray with all the strength I have that this won't be the case, and that this can reach you without consequence and that it is worth it to hear from me.

I was reunited with many members of the family on my arrival, including Kin Mou, who sends his love to you. I am happy to reassure you that they are all in good health and doing well enough for themselves here. One of my many brothers gave me a job in his factory, and I have worked there since my arrival.

You may have heard of the growing support for communism and the troubles here, but I want to put your mind at rest and tell you that the agitators have been dealt with and life has returned to how it was before in this vibrant and hectic city that is so full of life and so full of hope. I pity future generations, as Hong Kong is becoming overcrowded, and there is talk of stricter immigration control in the future. However, for our family, we are here and it has been good for us.

My life was enriched just over a year ago when I met a wonderful man. His name is Gai Kwong, and he is so very handsome. We have been dating since we met, and Mom, I have to tell you that I am very much in love. There is a problem though; he actually lives in a country called Canada, which is a long way away. He has had to return there because his father has suffered a stroke. Before he left, he asked me to go with him and marry him. Although I told him it was too sudden a decision, I have thought of little else since he departed.

I miss him terribly, and although the thought of moving so far away terrifies me, I feel that perhaps it is something that I must do to be with the man I love. What do you think Mom? Should I follow my heart once again, as I have always done throughout my life? If I go, it is doubtful that I will ever return, and the thought of never seeing you again is heartbreaking. I needed to tell you that I am seriously considering it, but it is not a decision I would take lightly. Although my final decision is not yet made, I already suspect where my future may be.

I wanted to thank you, Mom, for everything that you did for me all your life. You were a tower of strength when things changed so dramatically for us, and you battled on even after being so terribly ill. I greatly admire your determination and strength of will and I hope that I am even half the woman you are. I am truly sorry for the suffering I caused you by my actions, and desperately hope that you understood and supported my reasons.

I love you so much, Mom, and I miss you dreadfully. How I wish things could be different and how I hate the government for tearing us apart like this. I think of you every single day, and the thought of you comforts me but when I conjure up a specific memory it hurts so terribly I can hardly breathe. Please take care of yourself dear mother, look after yourself well and be proud of the family you have raised.

Your ever-loving daughter, Suk Hing

Tears ran down Suk Hing's face as she folded the letter and placed it carefully into an envelope. There was so much more she wanted to say, but she couldn't find the words. Writing wasn't her strongest ability, and the letter had taken all her concentration. She wished the words would flow easily; that she could pour her heart out onto the page and send it across the miles. Instead, she enclosed a check for two hundred dollars. Back in the town she had come from, two hundred dollars would be enough to support a person for approximately five years. The gesture would have to take the place of the things she couldn't say, and she hoped her mother would understand. She was still concerned that the letter might do more harm than good and before she could change her mind, she rushed out to mail it, holding it tight to her chest before finally letting it go.

Once the letter was sent and out of her hands, she felt like a great weight had been lifted from her shoulders. So many times, she had the opportunity to say those three small words to her mother, yet she hadn't done so, not since she was a small child. They had needed to be said, and now, finally, they were.

Chapter Twenty-Three

"Writing cannot express all words, words cannot encompass all ideas"

April 1971

Suk Hing carried on, working hard but thinking of nothing else of Gai and the possibility of travelling to a country that was truly foreign to everything she had known. One morning, she awoke and just knew. The time for hesitation and logical thinking was over; she needed to follow her heart. With renewed determination, she contacted Gai and excitedly told him that she would be honored to be his wife, and would gladly come to Canada to join him there. Their excitement and delight practically buzzed over the crackling telephone line.

It only took a day or so for Gai to get back in touch with her. He had made all the travel arrangements and she was to begin her journey to Alberta, Canada within the next few days. They spoke every day until that point, talking of their hopes and dreams for the future, how they would spend their lives together, where they would live, how they would raise their family in the future.

A few days before she was due to set out, Suk Hing received something special, something she would treasure forever. She carried it with her everywhere she went as she tied up all the loose ends in Hong Kong and said tearful goodbyes to the extended family she had rediscovered there.

Sitting alone on the long but thrilling journey to this new Promised Land and her brand new life of love and happiness, Suk Hing put her hand deep into her pocket. Her fingers found the familiar shape of Bui's pocket watch, which she had carried with her ever since their arrival in Macau. She held it for a moment and whispered something else half forgotten from her childhood:

"I let go of what I am, so I can become what I might be."

Letting the watch go, she rummaged further in her pocket and located the precise item she was looking for. She had handled it so much already; the paper was creased and dog-eared. The shakily scrawled Chinese characters swam in front of Suk Hing's eyes, the poorness of the writing an indication of how sick her mother had become since she had left her. Rubbing the tears away in order to focus and drying her wet hand on her clothing before grasping the sheets tightly, she read the words for the hundredth time.

My Dearest Little One

I was delighted to receive your letter and hear all about what had become of you and the family. It does this old, tired heart good to know that you are all well.

I want to tell you that I always understood your actions and supported everything you did. Do not worry about me or any of the hardships you think you caused me; I would have gladly suffered much more to ensure the happiness of my daughter.

It brings me joy to hear that your life has been good since you reached Macau, and that there is hope, despite these dark times. I am glad you have found a good man. Although I want to tell you not to rely on anyone but yourself for your own happiness, I know that you will make the decision that is right for you.

I want you to go. I hope that this reaches you before you embark on your next adventure, and when you set foot on to the new land, you don't look back. You go and make a better life for yourself. When you get there, you work hard and don't rely on anyone for charity. Do not forget your past, but do not let it haunt you. Never use your past as an excuse so that the evils that you have endured may not be in vain.

I am proud of you, and all that you have achieved in your life. Continue to bring me joy and pride by having a good life, always working hard, and being a good wife and mother to your new family.

It is peaceful here now.

Epilogue

Suk Hing arrived in Canada on August 15, 1971. She and Gai Kwong soon married and moved to Tofield, a small town in central Alberta, where the couple opened and built up a successful Chinese restaurant in the small town.

Sadly, the letter was the last time she would ever hear from her mother. One month and two days after her arrival in Canada, Suk Hing received word that her mother, Nim Ping, had passed away in her home with no family by her side. She had finally succumbed to her long illness on September 21, 1971 at the age of sixty-two.

Suk Hing and Gai Kwong went on to have two children and through their ups and downs lived a peaceful life together. Suk Hing never forgot her mother's words that she could make her proud by working hard and caring for her new family. She did exactly that.

They retired from the restaurant in 2010 and moved into a small condominium in Edmonton, Alberta's capital city. They have four healthy grandchildren that they see regularly. Chloe, Alyssa, Felix and Theodore are the apples of their eyes and keep them on their toes.

Suk Hing's full blood brother, Kin Mou, also moved to Canada in 1979 and lived happily there, raising one fine son. In July 2013, he was diagnosed with cancer. One year and three months later, Kin Mou sadly lost his battle with the illness. He passed away in hospital on September 23, 2014. He was survived by his widow, son, and his three-year-old grandson.

Suk Hing has no surviving relatives back in China. Those that remain are all now living in different parts of Canada and the United States. Out of the large number of siblings and half siblings she had, only four still survive to this day.

Unfortunately, after her arrival in Canada, Suk Hing lost contact with her friends Bui and Lum Jong. The last she had heard, they were both doing well and still living happily in Macau. Their whereabouts are unknown at this time. To this day, Suk Hing, my mother, still has the pocket watch that originally belonged to Bui and that he carried with him throughout their journey together. It now sits in a glass display case in the living room in my home.

The companions from her first escape attempt, Hai and Kang, were never heard from or seen again by Suk Hing. She still believes that they were captured on the beach that night and prosecuted for their actions. She never did find out their real names. The friend portrayed in this book as "Jin Jing" was actually a male friend whose name the author cannot disclose. He remained in China, and in 1997, Suk Hing went back to visit him. On her arrival, she discovered that his health was failing badly. The years of labour in hazardous conditions had taken too much of a toll on his health. The last correspondence Suk Hing received from his family was to let her know that he had passed away.

During the same trip, Suk Hing also visited her old family home. It was still standing, but only barely. There was hardly anything left of the large, sprawling complex her family used to own. The exterior had succumbed to years of neglect, and the interior was rapidly disintegrating from water damage. A large red letter painted on the main entrance indicated that the residence had been condemned and was scheduled for demolition in the near future.

Afterword

I wanted to write this book not only to honour my Mom's story and her individual struggle, but as a commendation to all those who lived and died throughout those trying times. Some scholars have estimated that during the era of 1958 to 1962, which is now known as The Great Leap Forward, around forty-five million people died due to mass starvation, beatings, executions and poorly implemented economic programs. To this day, the Chinese government have downplayed both the situation and the number of deaths, recording only a small fraction of the known, and the estimated unknown. As it stands, it is currently ranked as the highest death toll due to famine in recorded human existence, and is ranked second in the total number of deaths for any cause, behind only World War II.

Those that fled this terrible situation and made the journey across the water from China to British-ruled Hong Kong or the Portuguese-controlled Macau are now known as "Freedom Swimmers." Although this was never officially recorded, it is estimated that hundreds of thousands of people attempted to make the swim. Historians and scholars alike generally accept that for every one person caught and arrested by the Chinese government, four evaded the authorities. It was this influx of young, strong, mainland Chinese immigrants that fuelled Hong Kong and Macau's industrial sector.

It is thanks to my mom's courage, strength and bravery that I was born and raised in the beauty and freedom of Canada, and for this, I will always be grateful. I hope that this book serves to honour and remember all the Freedom Swimmers, both those who made it and those who didn't. Theirs is a story that should be told and never forgotten.